The Prayer Mountain

The Prayer Mountain

Exploring the high places of prayer

Brother Ramon SSF

CANTERBURY
PRESS
Norwich

© Brother Ramon SSF 1998

Bible quotations are from the *New Revised Standard Version*
of the Bible
© 1989, by the Division of Christian Education of the National
Council of the Churches of Christ in the USA

First published in 1998 by The Canterbury Press Norwich
(a publishing imprint of Hymns Ancient & Modern Limited,
a registered charity)
St Mary's Works, St Mary's Plain,
Norwich, Norfolk NR3 3BH

British Library Cataloguing in Publication Data

A catalogue record for this book is available
from the British Library

ISBN 1-85311-225-9

Typeset by David Gregson Associates, Beccles, Suffolk
Printed in Great Britain by Biddles Ltd, Guildford and King's Lynn

For
Michael and Molly Dowell
in gratitude and with affection

Contents

Introduction   *Vision, Training and Achievement*   ix

1   Mount Ararat   *New Beginnings*   1

2   Mount Moriah   *Suffering and Sacrifice*   15

3   Mount Horeb   *The Burning Bush*   28

4   Mount Sinai   *Shining Cloud and Darkness*   41

5   Mount Nebo   *Viewing the Promised Land*   57

6   Mount Carmel   *Consuming Fire*   69

7   Mount Tabor   *Transfiguring Light*   82

8   Mount Calvary   *The Victory of Love*   96

9   Mount Olivet   *Received into Glory*   112

10   Mount Zion   *The Kingdom of God*   122

Epilogue   *The Climb Ahead*   137

Notes   140

Introduction

Vision, Training and Achievement

By the end of 1992 there had been 485 ascents of Mount Everest, and 115 climbers had died in the attempt. What is this powerful evocation of mystery, wonder and awe which Mount Everest, together with many other mountain peaks and ranges, produces in the human heart?

There seem to be three stages in any life-enhancing and creative adventure that anyone undertakes. First there is the moment of *vision* in which one is confronted with a call or vocation presented to mind, ear, eye and heart, which is devastating in its power and undeniable in its challenge.

This is followed by a period of *training* – the giving of oneself to the asceticism and discipline contained within the visionary call. This applies as much to the scientist as to the musician, as much to the athlete as to the mystical man or woman of prayer. It may begin, as with me, in childhood, and may last for months, for years or for a whole lifetime – and then some more!

The goal of the vision is the *achievement* of the call. In the spiritual quest there is actual experience of union with God, in which the pilgrim is touched and enveloped by glimpses of glory – as the vision promised.

Yet this is only a partial achievement of the goal, for each attainment contains within itself the stimulus to further adventure and further achievement, until the object or goal of vision is realized to be far greater than anything the human imagination could have envisaged.

The spiritual journey is the life of penitence, grace and joy, leading to glory. The initiating vision may be the experience of evangelical conversion, or it may occur further along in the Christian life, at a moment of spiritual enlightenment. Such 'moments' may be part of a process, but there are often particular experiences of grace in which we feel illumined by the Holy Spirit.

These three stages of vision, training and achievement apply not only to the spiritual path, but also to the mountaineer, or to any creative discipline of mind or heart.[1] Let me illustrate them in terms of the mountain metaphor which we are pursuing in this book.

First, the initiatory vision. In 1921, the Royal Geographical Society and the Alpine Club of Great Britain mounted an expedition to survey the possibility of ascending Mount Everest, the highest peak in the world. George Mallory was the Alpine Club's foremost member, and 50 miles from Everest, just past Khamba Dzong, he noted: 'We are just about to walk off the map.'

Climbing above the Yaru Gorge he looked up at the Himalayas which were shrouded by monsoon clouds. He suddenly had an experience in which his frustration and doubts were swallowed up in the rapture of the moment in which he and his companions became the first Westerners to observe Everest in its full, awesome glory.

We were able to make out almost exactly where Everest should be; but the clouds were dark in that direction. We gazed at them intently through field-glasses as though by some miracle we might pierce the veil. Presently the miracle happened. A whole group of mountains began to appear in gigantic fragments. Mountain shapes are often fantastic seen through a mist; these were like the wildest creation of a dream. A preposterous triangular lump rose out of the depths; its edge came leaping up at an angle of about 70 degrees and ended nowhere. To its left a black serrated crest was hanging in the sky incredibly. Gradually, very gradually, we saw the great mountainsides and glaciers and arêtes, now one fragment, now another through the floating rifts, until far higher in the sky than imagination had dared to suggest the white summit of Everest appeared. And in this series of partial glimpses we had seen a whole; we were able to piece together the fragments, to interpret the dream ...[2]

When I first read this description, my mind and heart overflowed in longing and love for God. This, *this* is the mystery beyond all mysteries, which human language cannot begin to describe, but which is hinted at, glimpsed and indicated in the utmost, the highest, the most supreme in human art and love.

The human metaphor must break down and fall short of the divine reality. Even following the description above, in the perceptive and beautiful letters that George Mallory wrote to his wife so tenderly, there is this somewhat sad conclusion at the end of the expedition: 'As it is we have established the way to the summit for anyone who cares to try the highest adventure.'

From vision we turn to training. We cannot remain in the visionary world while the demands and responsibilities of our daily lives surround us. The vision remains true and valid – indeed, it is indispensable – but to attain what the vision promises means taking up the ascetic discipline of training. This is a mixture of illumination and struggle. Some fall by the way, others struggle on with hopes and fears; some take the athletic disciplines in their stride, others enter into the beginnings of glory in their earthly life.

This may be illustrated by a group of mountaineers who set off from the North Col camp below the summit of Everest in May 1922. They consisted of Geoffrey Bruce, a Gurkha officer, who had never climbed before, his regimental field aide, Tejbir Bura, and the Australian-born George Finch, the most accomplished mountaineer on the expedition. At 26,000 feet (7,925 metres), after immense struggle and valiant effort, Bura collapsed, and in spite of Finch storming at him, and Bruce exhorting him, he could not respond. Finch gives his account:

> There he [Tejbir] collapsed entirely, sinking face downwards on to the rocks and crushing beneath him the delicate instruments of his oxygen apparatus. I stormed at him for maltreating it, while Bruce exhorted him for the honour of his regiment to struggle on; but it was all in vain. Tejbir had done his best; and he has every right to be proud of the fact that he has climbed to a far greater height than any other native. We pulled him off his apparatus and, relieving him of some cylinders, cheered him sufficiently to start him with enough oxygen on his way back to the high camp.[3]

As we explore some of the biblical mountain scenes in this book we shall feel that we must identify ourselves with such collapse and failure. This may well be part of the way for us – collapse, recovery, renewal and on with the pilgrimage. The biblical giants had their own times of cowardice and failure, as well as their glimpses of glory. That they experienced doubts and conflicts should encourage us lesser mortals, for the light and darkness of their experience will clarify the journey for us, and enable us to get up and go on.

The third stage is that of achievement. Don't be beguiled by such words as attainment, summit and achievement, for there is no end to our journey. Achievement is glimpsed at every lesser peak; each contains within itself the stimulus to further courageous ascent and effort. When Sir Edmund Hillary and Sherpa Tenzing were the first to reach Everest's summit in 1953, there was that brilliant moment of awe, of achievement, of panoramic glory. This gave way to the gratitude and wonder at the remembrance of those who had gone before, those who had blazed the trail and given their lives in the attempt. This was followed by the realization that this was not the end, but the beginning of a new journey. This achievement, long sought and dearly purchased, became the basis of a new vision, where the edges of human pilgrimage and the life of the spirit blurred. Edmund Hillary's evaluation makes it clear:

> No one succeeds alone. We all, in a sense, climb on the shoulders of those hardy characters who have gone before. Even on the summit of Mount Everest I felt surprise that Tenzing and I should have been the lucky ones. And certainly for me the summit of Everest was a beginning, not an end. There are so many adventures to meet and challenges to overcome.[4]

I have a similar feeling taking up my pen to write of the mystical path to spiritual union with God in love – what a mountain! I am on the way; I have glimpsed the vision; I am pursuing the pilgrimage. But as I read the stories of those who have gone before, I am both grateful for their daring and amazed at the enlightenment they share. I am also ashamed of my own feeble response and achievement.

Using This Book

This book is not written for experienced mountaineers of the spirit, nor for saints! It contains a rough map of spiritual experience traversed by one footsore but enthusiastic pilgrim who wants to share his journey with others.

You will find in the chapters quite different attitudes and responses reflecting the various biblical climbers. Spiritual experience must be personal and intimate, yet there is a basic pattern which we would do well to observe. St John of the Cross drew a mountain map which has a straight, narrow path right up the mountain – direct, challenging and not easy. On either side are two inviting, easier and even amusing tracks, but they lead nowhere – or worse, into confusion. The biblical climbers in these chapters reveal the joy and the toughness of the direct path and their stories will illuminate our own.

Each chapter consists of:

- the mountain theme
- the scripture passage (to be read in its entirety)
- some chosen verses from the passage
- the story of the journey
- a prayer on the theme
- suggestions for thought and action.

The way is dangerous, but the vision has stimulated me. The glory has moved me and the flame has lit the touchpaper of my soul. What I have experienced I must share; what I have learned I must pass on – and I must brave the dangers and wonder of the ongoing climb.

If your heart is moved, if your mind is enlightened and if you feel the pull and quest of such a pilgrimage, then my efforts will have been rewarded. We shall surely meet on the mountain path, and you may be able to encourage me when my strength is ebbing, or I may lift you up and share my vision, so that we may continue together the struggle which leads at last to the mystery of the eternal Love.

Ramon SSF
The Society of St Francis

Mount Ararat

New Beginnings: Genesis 8:1–22

God remembered Noah and all the wild animals and all the domestic animals that were with him in the ark. And God made a wind blow over the earth, and the waters subsided; the fountains of the deep and the windows of the heavens were closed, the rain from the heavens was restrained, and the waters gradually receded from the earth … and the ark came to rest on the mountains of Ararat.

Seeing Things in Perspective

What a moment it must have been for poor old Noah and his family. He is dumb throughout the narrative, and here he is speechless in more ways than one. Standing on the summit of a mountain takes breath and speech away. The panoramic view gives rise to a new perspective and evaluation of the struggle and the experience, before the descent is attempted.

The tumultuous wind and swell had driven the ark to a mountain-top north of the Mesopotamian Valley. The traditional Ararat summit (16,969 ft) stands some 4,000 feet above the permanent snow-line, and these mountains were the highest known to the peoples of Palestine and Armenia.

After all the trials and struggles of facing a hostile world, and of standing alone among a seething crowd whose lives were given over to evil, moral wickedness and denial of God, he now stands alone again on the top of the world – an old man standing on the heights before his God. Only one who has been there can know the feeling.

When Chris Bonington was over 50 years old he answered the call of Everest, but not for the first time. On this occasion there was immense melancholy as he remembered the friends who had climbed with him in days gone by and had perished on the way. On 20 April 1985 he found himself just below the summit, crouched in a foetal position, crying in great gasping sobs of sadness and exhaustion, and yet with tears of fulfilment for a task completed for them as well as for himself. I thought of Noah when I read Bonington's description:

> It was time to look around. The summit is the size of a pool-table, but we could move about on it without fear of being pushed over the edge. To the west lay the Tibetan plateau, a rolling ocean of brown hills with the occasional white cap. In the east rose Kangchenjunga, a huge snowy mass, and in the west the great chain of the Himalaya, with Shisha Pangma, China's 8,000-metre peak, dominating the horizon. Immediately below us, across the western Cwm, was Nuptse, looking stunted now. To the south was a white carpet of cloud covering the foothills and plains of India. We were indeed on top of the world.[1]

When God brings us to the mountain-top it is time for reflection, and such a place puts things in perspective. Tears of sorrow must have mingled with tears of joy for Noah as he took a retrospective look at the judgement and devastation that had overtaken those who refused to hear his preaching, refused to turn from their evil ways, and dismissed his warnings, pleadings and tears on their behalf. If Noah had found room for the procession of creatures in the three storeys of his ark, he would gladly have opened the door to penitent human beings who are precious to God.

Mount Ararat 3

Let's look at the story as Noah builds his thanksgiving altar on Mount Ararat, and perhaps God will give us a perspective on our own lives as we evaluate the past, take an introspective look into our own souls and face the prospective challenge of new beginnings.

The Demonic Power of Evil

The Genesis story is not simply history, though its narrative form with names, measurements and sites makes us think of it in this way. We need to see the whole story from the mystery of endemic evil at the beginning of Genesis 6:1 to the rainbow sign of the Noahic covenant at Genesis 9:17. It is then possible to see that the whole story is on a cosmic scale, beginning with the mysterious forces of darkness that invade the human race, through to the judgement and salvation of the drowning flood, the saving ark and the covenant of mercy where the bow of vengeance and warfare is transformed into the rainbow covenant of promise. And this looks forward to the kingdom of universal peace.

The first eleven chapters of Genesis are pre-historical but filled with theological truth. The stories of a seven-day creation, Eden and Fall, Noah's ark and the Tower of Babel are all parables of sin and redemption, and though not strictly historical are theologically and existentially true, telling of the human condition under the judgement and mercy of God.

A great deal of the language of analogy is used in these chapters to speak of God (called *anthropomorphism*), for we have no other language to use, and perhaps the profoundest and most amazing statement of that kind is found in these words from Genesis:

And the LORD was sorry that he had made humankind on the earth, and it grieved him to his heart. So the LORD said, 'I will blot out from the earth the human beings I have

created – people together with animals and creeping things
and birds of the air, for I am sorry that I have made them'
(6:6).

After the story of judgement and salvation has been told, we
then read:

> And when the LORD smelled the pleasing odour [of
> sacrifice], the LORD said in his heart, 'I will never
> again curse the ground because of humankind, for the
> inclination of the human heart is evil from youth; nor will
> I ever again destroy every living creature as I have done'
> (8:21).

Here is the unchanging, impassible, sovereign God feeling
sorry, changing his mind, losing his patience, indulging in
almost universal judgement; then smelling the sweet sacrifice
and repenting of what he has done, determining never to do
it again.

There are times in some Old Testament narratives and
legal judgements when God appears fickle, bad-tempered,
unjust, full of vengeance and penal retribution – altogether
inferior to the best of the creatures he has made. That is why
we need to be careful as we read the Bible, and ensure we see
Christ as the centre and prism through whom the revelation is
interpreted.

Some of the biblical writers – representing prophets,
priests and theologians – did project the human image,
clothing God with the failings and limitations of human
judgement, so that the deity did not rise higher than their
contemporary moral mores and norms, and we still do that
today.[2] We must differentiate between what human beings
think God is like (or want him to be!) and the revelation of
God's love in Christ. The revelation is always greater, wider
and deeper than our understanding, and God's love always
surpasses human thought or imagination.

In my own pilgrimage, theology and spirituality have mingled in the process. The more I have thought and prayed with the mystical tradition, and spent time with the scriptures in the presence of God, the more I have learned of the exceeding sinfulness of sin, and the ecstatic heights of the divine Love. This means that I have had to take both more seriously. I now understand the nature of sin on three levels:

- as human fallenness, failure and the rejection of the good;
- as massive psychic forces which are corporate in their operation, such as international warfare or the oppressive nature of totalitarian political regimes;
- as 'the mystery of iniquity' which perpetrates torture, holocaust and genocide in our world, energized by demonic powers of darkness in the spiritual realm (see Ephesians 6:10–17).

On the other hand, I have entered into the divine Love at such a level as to experience myself as loved and embraced by the compassion of Christ, and increasingly drawn into that love which releases me from isolation and purely individual participation. This links me with the communion of saints and into a corporate participation in the nature of God in the trinitarian community of Love.

All this means that the judgement of God is real and severe, but it is always within the context of mercy and reconciliation. The divine wrath is exhausted by the divine Love, and even on earth judgement is tempered by mercy.

That is why I call Ararat the mountain of perspective and new beginnings, for the covenant which God made with Noah is not exclusively for Jew or Christian, for he was neither. Rather, it was for humankind. For Noah, Mount Ararat was a new beginning because it was a new revelation of God, embracing the whole of human and creaturely life.

This was for our mortal state, with the promise of something beyond Noah's imagination in the salvation history of God's people.

The Ararat story really starts at the beginning of Genesis 6, where we find a strange mythical story of angels and demigods having sexual intercourse with mortals. The story is common to various mythologies, but instead of the episode ending in the immortality of the hybrid offspring, judgement is decreed with the shortening of human life. The intertestamental book of Enoch takes this story as the origin of human sin. This is also the kind of thinking behind Jude 6 and 2 Peter 2:4.

The reason for such a passage in the story of Noah is to emphasize the cosmic nature of evil which is at loggerheads with God. Evil has become an endemic, supernatural, monstrous disease that has infected heavenly beings and humankind. It is a poison at the heart of creation, like a life-threatening cancerous growth that has to be surgically cut away.

The description in v. 5 below not only pictures the days of Noah, but also puts us in mind of all the holy wars, jihads, crusades of ungodly religious people, and the demonic practices of Attila, Hitler, Stalin and the terrors and tortures of archipeligos and holocaust:

The LORD saw that the wickedness of humankind was great in the earth, and that every inclination of the thoughts of their hearts was only evil continually.

Those words could have been written over large periods of the twentieth century. The philosopher Isaiah Berlin called it 'the most terrible century in Western history', confirmed by what the novelist William Golding calls 'the most violent century in human history'. Such words are spoken in the light of scores of millions who perished under the now collapsed

Marxist regime of the old USSR, and the tens of millions who died under the Nazi dream of power and domination.

Such horrors continue in the massacres of Rwanda-Burundi, and the present complexities of the former Yugoslavia. This is not the whole truth, of course, but the musician Yehudi Menuhin expresses the century's perplexities when he says: 'If I had to sum up the twentieth century, I would say that it raised the greatest hopes ever conceived by humanity, and destroyed all illusions and ideals.' If we think we are out of the worst horrors, note this prophetic word written by Alexander Solzhenitsyn in 1993:

> Although the earthly ideal of Socialism-Communism has collapsed, the problems it purposed to solve remain: the brazen use of social advantage and the inordinate power of money, which often direct the very course of events. And if the global lesson of the twentieth century does not serve as a healing inoculation, then the vast red whirlwind may repeat itself in entirety.[3]

There is a prophetic gloom and hopelessness which we must be careful not to fall into here, which could be buttressed by certain theological doctrines of the total depravity of our humanity that are neither biblical nor true to our whole experience. We shall see that the broad teaching of this Genesis passage will teach us that the *imago Dei*, the image of God in the human spirit, has not been entirely obliterated. But it is certainly twisted, marred, broken and in need of redemption. Noah represents the godly remnant which hold back the dark powers.

The strange, demonic verses which introduce the sixth chapter set the scene, and indicate that the dark perversions of the human spirit which led to moral bankruptcy in Noah's day are energized at source by the malevolent powers which are set against the mercy and justice of the living God. William Neil comments on this passage:

It is to man in this hapless plight that the Bible speaks. But it demands that first we recognise ourselves as we are and the world as it is, that we see in desperation and disillusionment the hopelessness of our case. Man cannot save himself. No human panaceas, educational, scientific or social, can remedy our situation for we have 'to struggle not with blood and flesh but with ... the potentates of the dark present, the spirit-forces of evil in the heavenly sphere' (Ephesians 6:12).[4]

The Faithful Remnant

Even as I write these words and consider the judgement of God upon all unrighteousness that confounds and contradicts the law of love, I hear the joyful singing of the Negro Spiritual: 'But Noah found grace in the eyes of the Lord'. Noah is in the line of the faithful men and women in every age, and the list is found in the heroes of faith in the eleventh chapter of the Hebrew epistle: 'By faith Abel ... by faith Enoch ...' and:

> By faith Noah, warned by God about events as yet unseen, respected the warning and built an ark to save his household; by this he condemned the world and became an heir to the righteousness that is in accordance with faith (v. 7).

Noah is in the line of the biblical heroes of the Jewish and Christian tradition which continues through Abraham, Isaac, Jacob and the prophetic line of Israel. It is taken up in the New Testament apostles and martyrs, and comes to fulfilment in the Suffering Servant and Messiah Jesus, through whom the world's salvation is accomplished.

Noah himself is neither Jew nor Christian as we have said. He represents humankind more widely simply because he is human. He is the righteous man who seeks God by the inward law written in his heart and conscience (Romans 2:15), and in this sense points not only to those in the Jewish-

Christian tradition, but also to the godly and righteous, whether Hindu, Sikh, Muslim or Buddhist.

Noah illustrates the biblical principle whereby the obedience of the one is the means of the salvation of the many; the principle that lies at the heart of the gospel where Christ is Saviour, Mediator and Redeemer for all humankind. The theology of Noah's ark is that humankind may be corrupt and lost, deserving of the divine anger, but through the grace of God and the obedience of Noah, for the sake of that good man, his family survive the deluge of the flood, in order to begin again as saved sinners and redeemed men and women (cf. 1 Peter 3:20–21).

The theologian who painted the dark picture of the depravity of humankind in Genesis 6:1–7 could not help but cry out with relief at the end of that description: 'But Noah found grace in the sight of the Lord.'

Before we conclude that the whole mass of the human race is to be damned and a tiny remnant of the elect is to be saved, let us recall that the end of this story of mass destruction in the deluge of drowning simply failed, and God was sorry that he had done it, and purposed never to do it again! This is the writer's way of saying that there is a better way, that the remnant is there not simply to be the elect, but that they are elected to be a light to the nations (Isaiah 42:6; 49:6).

That is what the story of Jonah is all about. Neither the elect Jews nor the elect Christians are called apart from the rest so that the latter may be damned – that is a caricature of the gospel. Election is to service, and although Jonah's theology made him want God to damn the gentile Ninevites, God wanted to save them. When Jonah suspected that God wanted to save them through the preaching of his elect prophet he got very angry.

The flood story is told as a parable[5] to show that this is *not* God's way of dealing with the world – for it failed, and God himself is pictured as having pity upon the sinfulness of humankind and purposing in his heart not to destroy his creatures like that again. This resulted in the Noahic Covenant for all people, which made possible a certain stability, law and order in a sinful world until the time of grace in Christ should come.

One of my fellow writers for the Bible Reading Fellowship notes dealt with these chapters earlier this year.[6] He said that when his son, as a child, heard the story of Noah he was shocked. 'That isn't our God, is it, Daddy?' the child asked. He was right, and the theologian of Genesis agrees, for the story is told in order to show that this way of dealing with human sin – simply to damn and exterminate – is not God's way. The BRF note is worth quoting:

> The tale of the great flood, one of many flood-stories from that part of the world, becomes a parable of God's response to human sin. Whatever he decides to do about the evil inclination of humanity, he will not simply give up and wipe away his creation. As long as the earth lasts, God will send his rain upon the just and the unjust alike.

God's Judgement and God's Mercy

I do not want the reader to think that God does not judge and deal with sin. He does. Indeed, the man or woman who knowingly, purposefully and boastfully gazes into the face of the divine Love and rejects it, is judged ... is lost ... and ultimately is not among the saved. For even God will not save one who adamantly does not want to be saved. But such people will not be damned and tormented for ever in a flaming hell!

If they reject love, light and truth, they will fall back into unloving, darkness and error; they will lapse into non-being, which is the opposite of what God offers them in Christ: fullness of life in glory. All the pictures and symbols of such lostness in the New Testament do represent a real situation, but that situation ultimately becomes the outer darkness of annihilation. For if there could be a place or state that ultimately existed in rebellion against God eternally, then the dualism would never end, the divine Love would never be victorious and God would never be 'all in all' (1 Corinthians 15:28).

The covenant that God made with Noah is for all people, and it represents the God who, in spite of human sinfulness and rebellion, takes this into account and still gives stability in nature, and imparts a basic law to enable human decency to operate between people, with the promise that God will not obliterate humankind (Genesis 8:21–9:17).

The Noahic covenant is not the covenant of grace that we have in Christ. Noah was a just and righteous man, but he was not a perfect man. Life after the flood would still be imperfect and sinful, but there now exists a covenant of mercy. God's natural covenant with Noah is simply to make human relations possible until the New Covenant of grace in Christ appears. It recognizes that there is a certain fear in relationships between human beings and creatures of the natural order. God provides a beautiful and ordered universe, but recognizes the fallen condition. Humans kill for food and, not being able to trust their neighbours, put regulatory laws into place in order to keep people on the straight path by fear of the consequences. Capital punishment is tolerated for the taking of human life – but all this is *not* what God intended it to be.

Nevertheless, even though this became a different world from God's intention, it was still his world. God set up the legal regulations that governed human and creaturely relations in a fallen world, yet men and women still bore his mark and image. This eventually led to the concept of the state with its restraining influences of law and order. Organized government at best (though itself easily corrupted) is meant as a dam against the flood of disaster, and is a blessing from God, and is to be respected and obeyed. Christians of the New Covenant are not under law, but under grace, but even they are citizens of the state at large and must reverence state order. The New Testament attitude to the state is found in Romans 13:1–7 and 1 Timothy 2:1–3, reflecting Paul's awareness of the principle of order in place of chaos. But when the state itself begins to persecute the people of grace then it is called antichrist, and this set of circumstances is found in the book of Revelation.

The world under law recognizes that people do not respond to one another and to God in spontaneous love, but that compromises and second-best are involved in family and individual relationships, in politics, commerce and in international relations. The machinery of government is based on mutual self-regard, and politics becomes 'the art of the possible'. Often things are not possible, and war is the result. All such things are recognized in the covenant with Noah, in the fabric of civilized life. But that lovely verse 'Noah found grace in the sight of the Lord' means that there is always a remnant, a minority, of upright, moral, righteous people who are the leaven in the body politic.

They may or may not be of the Judaeo-Christian tradition, and they are certainly not sinless, but they are relatively just, and through them God moves by his universal Spirit, as far as our fallen society allows. But for these people, human life and relations would fall into chaos, and by the mercy of God human life continues in this second-best way. But it is a fallen world, where selfishness and consumerism often rule, where the market economy, power of law and fear of prohibition is the best that can be expected.

This is the world-system which has forfeited Paradise, and this is why our best attempts in families, communities, religion and state so often fail. All our attempts are dogged by frustration, so that our best politicians are unable to bring peace to troubled nations or reconciliation to communities torn apart by strife.

But that is only half the story, and the rainbow in the cloud is the sign of peace in place of the bow of vengeance and rivalry. The rainbow is a promise, and the whole of the Old Testament reflects the best that law can do. But there is a promise that God will break through with the hope of redemption and deliverance in the future.

We shall travel, on our mountain pilgrimage, with Abraham, Moses and the prophets, and they will lead us to the Suffering Servant Messiah. The world-system of Church and state will take and crucify him, for that is what the system does to the Saviour. But that is not the end. Christ comes with the New Covenant of grace, rooted in the ancient covenants with Noah, Abraham and Moses, but bringing something entirely new. He is the new Noah, providing the ark of salvation for those who will come aboard.

God will not be content with the Noahic covenant, restraining by the rule of law and imposed from above. He did not create us to live under the authority of government as servants and slaves, but to respond in the freedom of sons and daughters in the family of love.

Noah stood on the summit of Mount Ararat and looked back on the sad rebellion of humankind. He acknowledged the particular grace that had delivered him and his family in the ark of salvation, and he realized that this was a place of new beginnings.

The bow in the cloud promised that there would be renewed covenants, and a long journey back to Paradise, but that somehow, he knew not how, God would completely restore the way back to his loving heart.

Noah believed and acted by faith, and it brought him to the summit of Mount Ararat. Today you stand on the top of your Mount Ararat, looking back, perhaps in sorrow and gratitude, and from this height you are called upon to look up to the God who has brought you there, and who calls you on in faith and love.

Prayer

Lord God of judgement and mercy: As I stand upon the mount of new beginnings, grant to me the perspective of grace; help me to see that unaided I cannot walk the way of truth.

Then let me look at the loving life and reconciling death of the Lord Jesus and find in him my new beginnings, a life of grace and freedom, beginning with your forgiving love. Amen.

*

Action

Recognize that the covenant of works and law operates in the world of humankind, but that you have entered into the New Covenant of grace in Christ.

Allow the joy and freedom of the New Covenant to enter into your life today, beginning with family, and into school, job, church and neighbourhood. And what about politics? List ways in which you and your friends can make this possible, and resolve to get them under way.

2

Mount Moriah

Suffering and Sacrifice: Genesis 22:1–19

After these things God tested Abraham. He said to him, 'Abraham!' And he said, 'Here I am.' He said, 'Take your son, your only son Isaac, whom you love, and go to the land of Moriah, and offer him there as a burnt-offering on one of the mountains that I will show you.'

… And Abraham looked up and saw a ram, caught in a thicket by its horns. Abraham went and took the ram and offered it up as a burnt-offering instead of his son. So Abraham called that place 'The LORD will provide'; as it is said to this day, 'On the mount of the LORD it shall be provided.'

God Contradicting Himself

This is a most beautiful, most moving, but most perplexing passage of scripture. In our last chapter, without any climbing, we were set down – within the safety of the ark – upon the summit of Mount Ararat. In our next chapter we shall find ourselves confined to the base of Mount Horeb. But here we have to do some climbing, and the Moriah path is beset by obstacles.

The reason for the climb increases our apprehension as we place one foot in front of another, for the demands made upon us when we get to the top are beyond anything we could have imagined. If we think of it as a kind of testing (and Abraham could not have been aware of that when he heard and obeyed), we could perhaps lay hold of a promise found in times of testing. But the fearful issues facing us in times of ignorance and darkness seem insuperable. It may be well for us to take note of one of the firm promises of scripture at the outset, for there are such contradictions presented in this story that we shall need some firm ground on which to stand. Here it is:

> No testing has overtaken you that is not common to everyone. God is faithful, and he will not let you be tested beyond your strength, but with the testing he will also provide the way out so that you may be able to endure it (1 Corinthians 10:13).

It is clear that you cannot simply pick a passage or proof-text from parts of the Old Testament and make it a basis for belief or moral practice. We are aware of that when dealing with passages in the warring and sanguine book of Joshua, or in the lists of prohibitions, regulations and abominations found in Leviticus. But there are narratives like the story of Mount Moriah, in which is mingled faith, obedience, affection, trust and a wild commandment to take a knife to slaughter and burn the child who is dearest to your heart. Not only that, but to do it in the name of the God who has given you the boy, together with the promise that his seed shall be the means of blessing through future generations.

It is true that there were times and religions where human sacrifice was practised, and it was thought that God demanded it. But anyone who intended such an act today would be confined in a psychiatric unit, and anyone who carried it out, with sincere religious motivation, would be accused of murder and imprisoned for life (or in some countries, executed).

One would think that this is the last story to be told to

children in Sunday School, but I remember that as a boy I held this story in special reverence, and heard sermons about it; though even in fundamentalist circles it was interpreted in a mystical and symbolic manner, so there was no need to think out its moral consequences. So let us try to walk in Abraham's steps as, with Isaac, he climbed Mount Moriah towards a moment full of terror and contradiction.

This is the supreme test of Abraham's faith and obedience, for he had cut himself off from his entire past when leaving Ur of the Chaldees, and now he is commanded to surrender his entire future. Here is the contradiction: the righteous God commands human sacrifice, and the loving father is asked to kill and sacrifice his son.

The outcome of such an obedience would be the cancellation and denial of the promise that God had made to Abraham; that through Isaac's seed much blessing would flow among the nations. In the following verses the contradiction is encapsulated: 'It is through Isaac that offspring shall be named for you' (21:12); and 'Take your son ... and offer him as a burnt offering' (22:2).

The promised son of salvation to the world is to be snatched out of history – and it is beyond all human reason and comprehension. The problem is contained in obedience to God's command in the face of hopeless despair. Can Abraham accept that the God who has given Isaac can take him away at his will and pleasure?

There is a certain tenderness in the whole moving passage, but we are not admitted to the confusions and perplexity of Abraham's heart. What we do see is the unquestioned obedience: 'So Abraham rose early in the morning ... and his son Isaac ... On the third day Abraham lifted up his eyes and saw the place afar off' (22:3–4). Not a word is spoken.

In intention Isaac is offered; the boy is dead. But what anguish and abandonment must have filled Abraham's soul as he laid the wood upon the boy's back, took the fire and the knife (so that Isaac would not hurt himself?), and faced

the mountain on the ascending path. Perhaps he remembered
the words spoken by the Lord about Isaac's birth in the face
of Sarah's unbelief: 'Is anything too wonderful for the
LORD?' (18:14). He was well practised in believing against
hope, and perhaps such an attitude strengthened him as he
walked. But suddenly the voice of the boy broke in upon
his thoughts:

> 'Father!' And he said, 'Here I am, my son.' He said, 'The
> fire and the wood are here, but where is the lamb for a
> burnt offering?' Abraham said, 'God himself will provide
> the lamb for a burnt offering, my son.' So the two of them
> walked on together (22:7f.).

They arrived at the appointed place. Abraham prepared the
altar, laid the wood in order and bound Isaac. (Does he
explain, console or justify, and are there tears? And the boy –
does he resist, surrender or show fear?) Then Abraham took
his knife, lifted it glinting in the sunlight, and suddenly – in
that awful and opportune moment – the voice of God
sounded loudly and clearly in ear and heart: 'Abraham,
Abraham!' And the order is countermanded, faith is assured,
the promise restored, and father and son are reunited in the
strange mystery of the mountain.

Abraham then heard a struggling or a bleating, and he
turned and saw a ram caught by its horns in a thicket, so
he offered it upon the same altar in the place of his son,
and called the name of the place 'The LORD will provide'.
Then the Lord spoke again through his Angel and reaffirmed
all the promises of seed and land, now with universal
application:

> 'By your offspring shall all the nations of the earth gain
> blessing for themselves, because you have heard my voice'
> (22:18).

Levels of Meaning

When I was 14 years old, the eighth verse of Genesis 22 arrested me: 'God will provide *himself* a lamb for a burnt offering.' The transposition of the word indicated that God *himself* was to be the lamb, and I understood it as a prophetic insight of Abraham, for that translation is found in the Authorized Version which I used exclusively. The Old Testament was read in conjunction with the New, and my understanding was supported by Hebrews 11:17–19:

> By faith Abraham, when put to the test, offered up Isaac. He who had received the promises was ready to offer up his only son, of whom he had been told, 'It is through Isaac that descendants shall be named for you.' He considered the fact that God is able even to raise someone from the dead – and figuratively speaking, he did receive him back.

Any problems with the text and with the morality implied did not trouble me then as they would later when I constructed problems for myself by insisting with my fundamentalist peer group that the text was infallible, and that there was a kind of flat level of inspiration throughout the Bible.

The problems of God seeming to tempt Abraham to sin, hiding his smiling face behind a frowning providence, willing human sacrifice, together with his direct word of command for some of the horrific massacres of the book of Joshua and other military and prophetic expeditions of violence and bloodshed – all these piled up as I sorted out my theological stance.

Nevertheless, the power and inspiration of both Old and New Testament scripture spelled out their own authenticating validity in my evangelical experience. I could not deny its dimension of reality and joy in God, and it gradually became clear that there was a kind of progressive revelation operating at various levels throughout the Bible, and that the love of God in Christ was the vantage point and prism through which all scripture should be read and interpreted. Skill and intuition were needed to negotiate this particular mountain!

In our passage, as in many others, texts that are thousands of years old have to be read with a certain latitude and insight into the moral mores of the times. Also the different sources and redactors on the text have to be considered with their particular theological insights and preferences.

It was clear, for instance, that human sacrifice was practised generally in Canaanite fertility cults, and children were passed through the fires of the god Molech. Such practices were abhorrent to the Israelites and there was direct legislation against it (Deuteronomy 18:10). In later days king Josiah destroyed the Topheth shrine where child sacrifices to Moloch had taken place (2 Kings 23:10).

Whatever else one makes of the testing of Abraham, it is clear that this passage replaces *child* sacrifice by *animal* sacrifice. The high point of revelation in the Old Testament sacrificial system is where Micah asks how God should be approached in worship, and then answers that it is not with a multiplication of calves or rams, nor with rivers of oil, and continues:

> Shall I give my firstborn for my transgression, the fruit of my body for the sin of my soul? He has told you, O mortal, what is good; and what does the LORD require of you but to do justice, and to love kindness, and to walk humbly with your God?

If we take on such discrimination and discernment in reading Old Testament scripture we shall be able to enter into that world and see the relevance and application of some of the narratives, prophecies and parables that are written for our instruction (Romans 15:4).

Messianic Significance of Isaac

Our passage is included in the paschaltide readings on the suffering of Christ, and although we need not follow the allegorizing of St Augustine in such details as the ram caught in a thicket symbolizing Christ wearing the crown of thorns, the reading and interpretation of this passage has always led the Church to see its messianic implications.

It is clear that the passage quoted above from Hebrews 11:17–19 shows that in the Early Church Isaac was seen as a messianic type of Christ, and that God raised Christ from the dead in order that the promise to Abraham should be fulfilled in Christ and his Church (Galatians 3:16).

There is a direct line of thought between Abraham, the father of the faithful, and the Messiah (Matthew 1:1); all who believe in Christ are sharers of Abraham's faith (Galatians 3:7). Isaac is the firstfruit of the promise, and Christ identified himself with Isaac when he said 'Abraham rejoiced that he would see my day; he saw it and was glad' (John 8:56).

Isaac was the beloved son of Abraham, just as Christ was of his Father, both born by grace and miracle. As Isaac took up the wood of the sacrifice, so Christ willingly took up his cross, on the road of suffering. Both were the children of sacrifice, willing to lay down their lives and thereafter rising from the dead (Hebrews 11:19). The loving Father was willing to surrender his obedient Son in costly sacrifice (Romans 8:32), and as Abraham's faith was vindicated, so was Christ's,

> ... who for the sake of the joy that was set before him endured the cross, disregarding its shame, and has taken his seat at the right hand of the throne of God (Hebrews 12:2).

Moriah, Mount of Suffering and Sacrifice

Such a climb as Abraham made with Isaac comes to us in various ways. We can become appalled and desolated by the suffering laid upon a loved one in terminal illness; we can be beaten down by a depression in which there seems to be no light at the end of the tunnel; we can struggle with burdens laid on us by our genetic structure or our circumstances. In all these situations, set in a world in which old age, poverty, sickness and disability are often ignored or ill-treated, it is no wonder that we question the goodness and the love of God.

As Christians we are not exempt from any of these perils; sometimes it seems as if we are more prone than others to some of them. We read our scriptures, sing our hymns, and sigh over their meaning:

> Judge not the Lord by feeble sense,
>   But trust him for his grace;
> Behind a frowning providence
>   He hides a smiling face.

The frowning providence is frequently in evidence, but the smiling face seems no longer to shine, making us feel that God certainly moves in mysterious ways.

The story of Mount Moriah fits us well. All the glorious promises seem to have faded, those we love are suffering, our loneliness wraps us round and the world is hostile. Even as I write these words a whole procession of friends are before me: the young mother who composed her deed of care for the baby she was leaving behind as she died of cancer; the young wife whose husband and two young boys were dumb with grief as they witnessed her suffering; the Elim missionary who, at the height of his ministry in a progressive African country, was struck fatally with a brain tumour; the missionary nurse who contracted AIDS from a dying patient; the young father whose little girl is autistic and dumb.

These are a few who immediately come to mind, for they have been part of my recent prayers and tears. And with them there are those who have wept with me in my hermitage chapel for themselves, for their loved ones and for situations in which it is impossible to discern the will of God or the possibility of love or healing.

How, then, is it possible – faced with these personal sorrows, and aware of their multiplication in individuals and nations throughout the world – to continue ascending the path of pilgrimage? Can we close our eyes to it all and keep on repeating theological party clichés? Can we affirm faith in darkness when all about us seems to deny its reality? Do we keep on cheering in our evangelical or catholic ghettos, keeping each other's spirits up while we are surrounded by the world's engulfing darkness?

Abraham: A Pattern of Faith

If we closed our hearts and minds to the sorrows of the world we would not be Christians; if we surrendered faith and trust under suffering we would not be in the great line of simple believers down through the ages who have borne their glorious witness. They may have been persecuted, ill treated and martyred, but they have also found forgiveness, healing and deliverance, and have sung psalms of praise and trust in the darkness. There is light in our darkness, and it is not simply the case that we should discover it, rather, we should learn so to live or die in its warmth that its radiance and compassion should flow through us to all those who suffer in our world.

The terror and desolation that marked the first half of our Bible passage hid a profound faith that was rooted in the goodness of God, despite all appearances. Abraham had obeyed God in the years past by leaving his homeland, not knowing where he was going. He followed the mountain path by faith, not sure whether the goal or simply the journey was God's will. When there was no rational sense in the promises God made, 'he received the power of procreation, even though he was too old – and Sarah herself was barren – because he considered him faithful who had promised'

(Hebrews 11:11). Then he came at last to his greatest test: an obedience of faith in which everything seemed to be threatened, and the son of his love was to be offered in a sacrifice which was beyond all reason and meaning.

The eleventh chapter of the Epistle to the Hebrews is a primary witness to the fact that the blood of the martyrs is the seed of the Church. The story of the people of God is one of persecution, suffering and martyrdom – yet the onlookers and persecutors were astounded because such treatment was not only expected but accepted. God's presence is experienced right in the middle of trial, and there is singing as the martyrs yield their spirits to God.

Last week, an Anglican friend told me that he had been to visit his dying Catholic friend. There was a radiant acceptance in the dying man who thanked his friend for being with him, and he said: 'Victor, you have accompanied me in my dying – I shall accompany you in yours.' This week I received a letter from Mark about the death of his beloved stepmother, Vi. We had been holding her in faith for months and moving with her, in prayer, towards a good and gentle death. He writes:

Travelling with Vi in her journey towards physical death was a profound and valuable experience. I was fully involved from the beginning: talking to my Dad immediately after the initial diagnosis; sitting with him while Vi was in the operating theatre; visiting every day in the hospital; after chemotherapy treatments; later helping to support the visiting team as Vi became weaker at home; holding her hand as she lay semi-conscious and unable to eat; saying goodbye five minutes after she had died. The business is desperately sad, stressful and hugely tiring. It is also a privilege and, in a way, a joy to anticipate with a close friend, whose faith is growing in anticipation of her physical death, the whole realm of life beyond our present horizons.

Mark and his father, Ted, are coming to Glasshampton soon to share it all with me, and I know we shall take up the threads of our prayer and fellowship. Not only was Vi's faith gentle and firm right to the very edge of death and beyond, but the family are also now experiencing the comfort of God, and together we shall look into the future and take up the fact of Vi's death as part of the whole vision of where we are and the direction we shall take.

That procession of friends in real trouble I mentioned previously – out of their experiences of sorrow has emerged a mingling of joy. The God of all comfort has given them new hope for present life and future pilgrimage. I have tried not to evade the painful reality of our journey – it is, indeed, a stiff climb up the mountain – but I have also to bear witness to the frequent overcoming of suffering by the grace of the God who comforts us in our affliction.

But how is all this possible? I am not saying that a man or woman can believe what they like, live selfishly, behave towards family and neighbour despicably, ignoring the basic rules of health and compassion, and then, in deep trouble or a terminal diagnosis, expect God to extricate him or her by a quick fix of prayer or religion. That is not how Abraham behaved when he listened to what God was saying!

At each stage of his life he made a simple but profound act of faith, listened for the word of God and obeyed it. As he gazed upon the stars in the firmament and studied the wide desert around him (Genesis 22:17), he built up his life of prayer, and sent down contemplative roots into the soil of God's Holy Spirit. This discipline went on for years until it became a spontaneous and prayerful pattern of life.

With such a spiritual root-system beneath the surface of his external life he began to be aware of growth as he responded to the sunshine and rain of God's providential care. He began to bear leaves, blossom and fruit, so that when times of difficulty and darkness overtook him, and especially when that moment of terrible testing confronted him, he was able to act from that deep life in God that he had nurtured over the years.

You are on the mountain track of Moriah and the way is beset by stones, thorns and briars. The going is hard and there seems to be an ambiguity about its summit – a mystery and a terror. What you have to do in the present, as I hope you have been doing up to now, is to consolidate your life of prayer, and keep building upon the solid foundation which is Christ. This is the advice of Jude in his epistle:

> You, beloved, build yourselves up on your most holy faith; pray in the Holy Spirit; keep yourselves in the love of God; look forward to the mercy of our Lord Jesus Christ that leads to eternal life (20–22).

We shall discover various ways of doing this as we continue our mountain journey, but the principle I am laying down now is that in order to face the sufferings and the joys of our present lives we must cultivate lives of prayer and meditation in a loving relationship with Christ.

The consequences of this will be that not only will we be able to step forward in faith – not knowing necessarily where it will lead – but also that we shall live in the foreign land of this world system with compassion and joy, looking towards the immediate future of fruitfulness and the further future of consummation in heaven.

Such a stance will be world affirming, in that you will live in the joy of the present, and world denying, in that you will bear bold witness against all that denies justice and peace. If Abraham is our pattern on this Moriah mountain path, we can conclude with this witness:

> By faith Abraham obeyed when he was called to set out for a place that he was to receive as an inheritance; and he set

out, not knowing where he was going. By faith he stayed for a time in the land he had been promised, as in a foreign land, living in tents, as did Isaac and Jacob, who were heirs with him of the same promise. For he looked forward to the city that has foundations, whose architect and builder is God (Hebrews 11:8–10).

Prayer

Heavenly Father: There are times when my life is beset by sorrows and difficulties, when believing is full of ambiguity and life seems no longer sweet, and trusting no longer easy.

In such times may the grace of your Holy Spirit flow from the roots of my poor praying, enabling me to trust, to pray, to rest in your love.

Abraham's pattern of faith sustained him in the greatest test of all. Let me learn and practise such a pattern in my own life. Amen.

✳

Action

Realize that as a Christian you will have experience of faith and growth, but that from time to time there will be periods of conflict, testing and downright doubt.

Set yourself the task of being open and honest in your belief and your life, and set in motion the practice of prayer and meditation on a daily and disciplined basis. Do this not as an insurance against the great testing time, but as a pilgrim and a loving child of God.

3

Mount Horeb

The Burning Bush: Exodus 3:1–17

Moses was keeping the flock of his father-in-law Jethro, the priest of Midian; he led his flock beyond the wilderness, and came to Horeb, the mountain of God. There the angel of the LORD appeared to him in a flame of fire out of a bush; he looked, and the bush was blazing, yet it was not consumed. Then Moses said, 'I must turn aside and look at this great sight, and see why the bush is not burned up.' When the Lord saw that he had turned aside to see, God called to him out of the bush, 'Moses, Moses!' And he said, 'Here I am.' Then he said, 'Come no closer! Remove the sandals from your feet, for the place on which you are standing is holy ground.' He said further, 'I am the God of your father, the God of Abraham, the God of Isaac, and the God of Jacob.' And Moses hid his face, for he was afraid to look at God.

Solitude and Wilderness

Horeb is the mountain of God. It can be used synonymously with Mount Sinai, or as a spur of that mountain. In this powerful passage Moses is in the wilderness at the back of the desert, the solitary place on the lower heights of the great mountain.

Mighty things will happen on the ascending slopes and on the mysterious summit of this mountain, but here today is the preparation, the confrontation with the God of the mountain, and the call that produces in Moses the symptoms of a 'called prophet'. This call will shake him to his foundations, cause him to tremble with astonishment, shiver with awe and fall down with naked feet and covered face before the amazing manifestation of the fiery God of wonders who makes himself known by his holy name. This name is one that is so holy that its four Hebrew consonants are called 'the sacred tetragrammaton'. The name is not even to be whispered by unworthy mortals, for it is the name of the ineffable God who reveals himself in fiery glory and yet remains hidden in the dazzling darkness of mystery.

We do not have to ascend the heights of Horeb to be blinded and dazed by the ethereal atmosphere, for heaven comes down and glory fills the soul when confronted with the living God on the lower slopes. If this happens at these lower levels, what will it be when we begin to ascend? Let us follow the direction Moses takes.

The first thing is solitude. We shall see that there are mountains upon which there is need for, and joy in, fellowship. But whenever there is the need for a profound confrontation leading to an awareness of vocation, it must be in solitude, within a certain wilderness, at the base of the mountain. Ramon Lull, the Franciscan evangelist, missionary and hermit knew that all his enthusiastic proclamations and all his brave missionary endeavours would come to nothing unless first of all he had prostrated himself before the holiness of God in abandoned consecration. Moreover, he knew that the soul's confrontation with God was only secondarily for service – it was primarily for the sake of love. In his meditations for hermits, *The Book of the Lover and the Beloved*, he wrote:

The lover longed for solitude, and went away to live alone, that he might have the companionship of his Beloved; for amid many people he was lonely.

Moses came to Horeb, the mountain of God. God had appointed a time, a place and a puzzling circumstance. The commentator Guniel says that the sheep were his guides. I suppose that is a very Franciscan comment for a Jewish context, but the Old Testament often uses the animal creation to open the eyes and ears of God's servants. Was it not Balaam's ass who saw and heard the angel, and led stupid Balaam to recognize the wisdom of the animal? (Numbers 22:22ff.)

How often I have realized that God has used certain people, certain creatures or certain circumstances to bring me to a place where he can confront me directly – so that there is no longer any evasion. We are past masters at burying ourselves in activities, deserving charities, committee meetings or noisy frenetic relaxations, so that we don't have to face ourselves – or God. And then we hear ourselves singing:

O speak to reassure me, to hasten or control,
O speak and *make* me listen, thou Guardian of my soul.

and God answers the prayer!

The Hebrew writer often avoids using the name of God directly, and in this passage there is a progression in which we read of the Angel of the Lord, and then the direct voice of God from the midst of the fire, leading to the revelation of God's secret name.

It begins with the perplexing sight that stirred Moses' curiosity, drawing him nearer until he felt the reverberations of the divine presence. A bush was burning – no uncommon sight in the hot desert scrubland – but this commonplace sight suddenly became uncommon because 'the bush was blazing, yet it was not consumed'.

These words in Latin, encircling the burning bush, make up the logo of the Church of Scotland. It is a brave church that takes such words and image to portray the essence of its life and witness. Part of my theological education at New

College, Edinburgh, and my ministry at Glasgow enabled me to experience at first hand some of the prophetic insights of Scottish theologians and preachers. They certainly understood the symbolism of the God who revealed himself in the blazing bush to Moses.

See the way in which the story unfolds: Moses in the solitude and silence of the desert sees the bush aflame; his attention is caught because the blaze is not abating; he turns aside to gaze upon it, and then he is astonished, confounded and filled with awe. He hears and obeys the divine command, casts his sandals away, falls down before the Lord and covers his face in reverential awe.

The Prophetic Call

Whenever God calls to prophetic service in the Bible there is a shape to that call. It goes like this:

1 A vision/confrontation in the context of sacred space (temple) or nature (desert, mountain).
2 The response, which is one of awe and godly fear leading to penitence, abasement and cleansing.
3 A profound sense of passivity and receptiveness.
4 A declaration of the content and purpose of the call.
5 Instruction as to the way it will be carried out.

All the great prophetic calls reveal such a pattern[1] and this continues into the Early Church in the conversion of Saul of Tarsus on the Damascus road. In the case of Isaiah (6:1–8), it was the temple and its liturgical splendour that were the context of the call. But in our passage it is the mountain and desert, the overarching sky and the images of nature which provide the place and the vehicle of God's communication.

We may not be called to such a nation-shaking task as Moses, or be numbered among the foremost of the prophets, but the pattern holds good for all of us. It is God's way to get us alone, and even if there are people around we shall feel the solitude of being alone with God. It may be in a sacred place, on retreat in a scene of natural beauty – in the country or by the sea – or even at the base of a mountain which towers above us in majesty and wonder. The mountain of holiness that we have to climb may, surprisingly, have its base in the marketplace of consumerism and idolatry, and the products of materialism may be the very things that reveal to us our own inadequacy and emptiness. When flaming holiness is manifested we shall be brought to a place of abasement, penitence and cleansing.

It was not a *burning* bush that was the means of Brother Lawrence's conversion at 18 years of age, but a tree putting forth its buds in the springtime. He was confronted, amazed and converted! For him this was God's place and time, and from that simple meeting with God in nature he lived 'practising the presence of God' and died a lay brother in the Order of Discalced Carmelites in Paris at the age of 80.

Your life story may be different from that of Moses or Brother Lawrence, but the pattern is the same, and it is repeated at different points and various levels in your life. Sometimes the sense of awe and wonder is the primary thing; at other times, it is a deep sense of penitence, or a feeling of such passivity that all you can do is to remain in a state of receptivity, allowing God not only to give you the strength to stand upon your feet (Daniel 10:9–19), but also to provide the dynamic that will fire and enthuse you in carrying out your vocation and commission.

For Moses, even the time was right. It had been many years since, as a young man, he had come across an Egyptian beating a Hebrew slave unmercifully. At that time Moses was a privileged member of the royal house of Pharaoh, though he knew himself to be one of God's chosen but oppressed people. Anger flared up within him and he took it into his own hands to intervene. He looked both ways, and then killed the Egyptian, burying his body in the sand. It soon became clear that the story had got out, and he made himself scarce. The Exodus account shows Moses running off into the desert for fear of Pharaoh (2:14f.), but the Epistle to the Hebrews takes a larger view: 'By faith he left Egypt unafraid of the king's anger; for he persevered as though he saw him who is invisible' (11:27).

The important thing is to act when the time is right. Humanly speaking we would call it synchronicity, but God calls it providence. Moses went into the desert towards Midian, and he could not sort out his motives – a mixture of fear and faith. But God was leading him, delivering him from his premature release of the Hebrew slave from the violence of the Egyptian, so that the whole nation could be redeemed. If we remain pliable in God's hands with a responsive passivity, he will order the time aright, preparing the way before us.

Paul Tillich calls attention to the difference between the New Testament words for time – *chronos* and *kairos*.[2] *Chronos* (e.g. chronology) is clock time, measured in quantity. *Kairos* is the qualitative time of the occasion, the right time, the time of maturity – in fact, God's time. Tillich's concern is to show how Paul and the Early Church affirmed that the time in which Christ appeared was the *right* time, the *kairos*, and how his appearance was made possible by a constellation of factors that were providential – for God is at work in history and pre-eminently in the coming of Christ.

Here, in the experience of Moses, he was delivered from the premature and impassioned action which would have led to his death (2:15), so that he might be prepared in the solitude and meditation of the wilderness years. At the burning bush, the *kairos* had come, and the bush burned without being consumed.

In writing these words I cannot help but reflect upon my own life, and acknowledge the numerous occasions in which the *kairos* presented itself simply, clearly and irresistibly. The one that is in my mind's eye now is that *kairos*-moment, at four o'clock in the morning, when I was 21 years old. I was on night duty at Sully Hospital on the Glamorgan coast. The full moon shone on the still sea, and from my third-storey ward it reflected in calm serenity upon the water.

At that very moment I felt it: an interior call that said 'You must serve Me in the Church of God'. There was no question about it. Immediately before writing the night report, I penned a letter setting the wheels in motion towards training for ordination. The time had come.

Look into your own life and recall such encounters. You may not magnify them to such proportions as Moses' encounter with the living God at Horeb, but in their own way they may express the *kairos* – the moment in which God lovingly, powerfully and disarmingly addressed your soul. And do not let it remain in the past. The reading of these words is a simple encounter which may turn the direction of your life. Has God been quietly moving in the background, beneath the surface and within the circumstances of your life, bringing you to face a certain question or a particular direction? Perhaps the *kairos* has come for you. And there will be others in the future, for you are not self-propelled if you live at the bottom of this mountain, and the mature time has come.

The Power of God's Name

In the ancient world, to know the name is to have power or influence over the person. This is a common way of thinking among primitive peoples. People who take new names for themselves at important moments like baptism, confirmation, marriage, ordination or monastic life are aware of the importance of naming. My own name, Ramon, was not taken simply because there was another brother with my baptismal name, but because I was enamoured of Ramon Lull, the thirteenth-century Franciscan scholar, evangelist, hermit and martyr. It happens to be a variation of my baptismal name anyway, which is all to the good for it preserves continuity.

In our text you will see that the power of the name is underlined. The name Moses itself means 'drawn out' (of the water), and this calls to mind the faith of his mother who placed him in the ark in the bullrushes (Hebrews 11:23). In our present text at the burning bush the twofold use of his name has a numinous quality:

> When the Lord saw that he had turned aside to see, God called to him out of the bush, 'Moses, Moses!' And he said: 'Here I am.'

Before God reveals his name to Moses with all the mystery that surrounds it, he calls Moses by name to elicit attention, response and obedience. Once Moses' mind and heart are concentrated, his sandals are thrown off and his face covered in reverence. Then God discloses not only his purpose of grace for the redemption of his captive people, but also his own name and nature as the faithful covenant God of his people.

First, he reminds Moses of the amazing grace of past days, of the mercy and providence that attended Abraham, Isaac and Jacob. Then he speaks of the present oppression and misery of the Israelites under the Egyptian heel, and his intention to liberate them by the hand of Moses.

Moses' trembling increases as he realizes his own inadequacy for such a task, and he asks two relevant and powerful questions which have reverberated down to our own day: 'Who am I?' and 'Who are You?'

The first, 'Who am I?', is not simply a question of unworthiness such as: 'Who am I, weak and insignificant, to carry out this immense task?' Rather, it is: 'Who am I in relation to the flaming light of glory that confronts me?', or alternatively: 'Who am I – a gnat in this consuming fire?'

The question of identity is one that has haunted humankind throughout its history, and it was from a deepening life of prayer that St Francis cried out: 'Who am I, and who are You, Lord?' When men and women have been challenged by the vision of a mountain peak rising high into the heavens, the response has had within it the quest not only for adventure and ambition, but also for identity. Here is mountaineer Jim Lester addressing this very question:

It has gradually dawned on me that there is possibly a fundamental split within the typical climber ... that his life involves some paradoxes, and that out of these paradoxes might come the energy and its channelling that makes the difference between a mountaineer and the rest of us. Some of these paradoxes, darkly glimpsed, are these: that he is basically introspective yet highly active in attempting to master the outside world; that he is basically humanistic but tends to choose a career dealing with abstractions or the impersonal world; that he is assertively individualistic yet shows a distinct tendency to idealize the Buddhist way of life in which Nepal immersed us. These may all be clues to a divided nature, an ambivalence, which most people experience as distinctly undesirable. Ambivalence seeks resolution. I have come to feel that one of the deepest attractions of mountaineering is its potential, for a time at least, to allow us to feel *whole*, pulled together, undivided, undistracted – in a word, *ourselves*. Searching for the right words I find these of Ortega y Gasset touching and highly relevant: 'Each of us is always in peril of not being the unique and untransferable *self* which he is. The majority of men perpetually betray this *self* which is waiting to be; and to tell the whole truth our personal individuality is a personage which is never completely realized, a simulating Utopia, a secret legend, which each of us guards in the bottom of his heart.' [3]

In his encounter with the immensity of God, Moses found that the question of identity was mingled in his own person with its roots in his people's spiritual pilgrimage. Who he was, was conditioned by who God was in his dealing with his people. God had been known as *El Shaddai* (God Almighty; Genesis 17:1), which had to do with the high mountain places, *El Elyon* (Most High God; Genesis 14:18), and the plural form *Elohim*. His nature and character were the basis of the revelation of his ways, and as the Israelites were to be like him, they were caught up in the progressive revelation of who he was.

The study of the divine name and the streams of tradition that make up the Pentateuch are intriguing, for there are differences of approach and emphasis. But in the text before us, the nature and use of the divine name *Yahweh* marks a new chapter in God's dealing with his people through his servant Moses. This is the God of covenant, liberation, redemption and promise.

When Stephen summarized the story of Israel before the Sanhedrin, he described Moses as 'instructed in all the wisdom of the Egyptians' (Acts 7:22). He had been taught the religion of Egypt with all its gods and goddesses, animal worship and cult of the dead. We may also assume that he would be aware of the unsuccessful attempt of Akhnaton, about a century before the Exodus, to reform the corrupt priesthood and religion of Egypt. Its basis was the substitution of the one god Aton, the sun, for the polytheism of the state religion of Amun. This attempt at monotheism was a short-lived failure, but some scholars have indicated its influence on Moses.

There is always continuity in our progression in faith, whether in belief or practice, but in the revelation of God to Moses at Horeb, grounded upon what had gone before, there was the beginning of an entirely new understanding of the God who is moved with compassion at the cry of his people, who redeems them from oppression and slavery, and accompanies them in light and fire through the wilderness to the promised land.

When we come to the name itself, God responds to Moses' question: 'What is his name?' with the words 'I AM WHO I AM'. The NRSV has an important footnote: 'I AM WHAT I AM or I WILL BE WHAT I WILL BE.' He is the unchangeable God, and yet is the God of 'becoming' in the experience of his people. This name *Yahweh* is made up of the four Hebrew consonants YHWH, which comprise the sacred *tetragrammaton*. It is connected with the verb *hayah*, 'to be'. So sacred and holy were these letters that in later days it was forbidden to utter them, and in the reading of scripture, whenever the reader saw the sacred *tetragrammaton*, the word *Adonai* (Lord) was spoken. In most versions today (e.g. AV, NIV, RSV, NRSV), whenever Yahweh occurs, it is replaced by the capitalized LORD.

The patchwork of theological growth in understanding the nature and character of God throughout the books of Moses, leads to the deepening insights of the great prophets Isaiah, Jeremiah, Ezekiel, Amos and Hosea. And as the Old Testament anticipated the coming of the Suffering Servant Messiah we find that the name of Yahweh is incorporated into the name of Jesus who is the new Joshua and Saviour of the world.

This great development of faith was implicit in the encounter of Moses with God at Horeb, leading to the Exodus from Egypt. The name Yahweh is the name of he who is, who will be and who causes to be, and into this conception all the later insights of the prophets find their place.

As God revealed his plan to Moses it became clear that the oppressed Hebrew slaves were to be called out of Egypt, as Abraham had been called out into the unknown, and they would need to trust God as the One who would liberate them and never forsake them. From this creative moment before the burning bush beneath the heights of Horeb a new dynamic is released. There will be much tribulation and suffering ahead, and many bitter lessons to be learned, yet the people of God will follow Moses. He, in turn, will follow the pillar of cloud by day and the pillar of fire by night, which will lead them at last into the promised land.

From the Bottom of the Mountain

God reveals himself in the common bush, in the scrubland of the desert on the lowest depths of the mountain. He reveals himself too on the twisting, ascending paths, when the winds blow, the mists descend and the storms engulf the climber. The time comes when the mountaineer begins to experience the rarified atmosphere of a different world, a new climate with its attendant dangers and glories. And above all these is the summit, from which height all below carries a new and different perspective.

Eventually, Moses had to climb through all these struggles and wonders, and at last was buried in an unknown grave below a mountain of mystery. But today, he is here for us at the base of Horeb, the mountain of God, on his face before Yahweh, but receiving sufficient grace and help to initiate the mighty redemption that would carry God's people out of captivity and on the way to redemption.

We have our own Horeb experiences that we need to learn well, for unless we begin correctly the whole journey will be perplexing and counter-productive. Look at that prophetic pattern again. Learn anew the meaning of reverence, godly fear and true penitence – all leading to a receptivity of spirit that listens to God's will for your life, and receives the strength of the Holy Spirit to carry it out.

It is time to leave the desert, having learned the lessons of Horeb, and to begin the next chapter in our pilgrimage with God.

Prayer

Lord God of Mount Horeb: Prepare my mind and heart for a meeting with you; speak to me in the simple circumstances of my life; give me a penitent heart and a living faith.

Then I shall respond to the call of your Spirit, and obediently walk in the way of your will, to your praise and my joy. Amen.

*

Action

Look for the revelation of God in the ordinary circumstances of life. Turn aside to look and listen to happenings and people, and anticipate God's coming in friends, in your job and in your church.

When this happens, work out practical ways of putting inspiration into action. Do not stay with resolutions or good intentions, but translate your faith actually to relieve suffering, actually to lift burdens, actually to be a more patient, joyous and receptive person.

4

Mount Sinai

Shining Cloud and Darkness: Exodus 19:16–20; 33:12–23; 34:28–35

On the morning of the third day there was thunder and lightning, as well as a thick cloud on the mountain, and a blast of a trumpet so loud that all the people who were in the camp trembled. Moses brought the people out of the camp to meet God. They took their stand at the foot of the mountain. Now Mount Sinai was wrapped in smoke, because the LORD had descended upon it in fire; the smoke went up like the smoke of a kiln, while the whole mountain shook violently. As the blast of the trumpet grew louder and louder, Moses would speak and God would answer him in thunder. When the LORD descended upon Mount Sinai to the top of the mountain, the LORD summoned Moses to the top of the mountain, and Moses went up.

Stages on the Journey

Moses at the foot of the mountain … Moses entering the cloud below the summit … Moses climbing deeper into the smoke and the darkness … then Yahweh descends to the summit and calls Moses into the deep darkness.

A trembling Israelite, watching from the bottom of Sinai and seeing Moses disappearing into the enveloping cloudy darkness, feeling the thunder-and-lightning-quaking of the mountain and hearing the crescendo of trumpet blasts, would fall on his face in confusion. Our place is to lie quietly beside him, sharing something of the awe and fear of the common people. But we must also, as far as we are able, ascend deeper into the dazzling darkness with Moses, and try to understand.

At the outset of our mountain journey we said that there seem to be three stages involved in any human discipline, adventure or life-enhancing quest. In mountaineering literature there are many references to the initial impact of what we may call *vision*, which may be an immediate impact or a concentrated period which impresses itself upon the young soul. This may come through a story told or read, a mountaineering film or still picture of a snow-capped mountain rising in solitary glory into the overarching sky. Or it may be the idealism and enthusiasm communicated by the figure of a lone climber or dedicated team struggling against the challenge of a mountain-face or peak. This moment or period of vision is the basic imprint which remains through glory and apparent failure, and which spurs one on to increasing effort and the overcoming of powerful obstacles.

The second stage consists of the period of *training*, in which the idealistic vision is tempered by the sheer physical and mental demands of getting into the gear, setting one's feet upon the slopes, and learning as an individual and part of a team that the romantic dream must perish. What takes its place is the basic know-how and effort of training, aided by guides and teachers who have been there before you, and know the way.

The third stage is one often anticipated and tasted during the slog of training, and may be thought of as *achievement*, when the peak or summit is reached, and the panoramic glory stretches out into seeming infinity. There are many lesser moments of achievement leading to the reaching of what was thought to be the goal or quest. But once there, even on top of the world, it becomes clear that *this* is not the goal, and the holy grail remains out of reach.

As I've been exploring some of the mountaineering literature and photography I found myself over and over again being reminded of the mystical quest for union with God. The classic pattern of *purgation*, *illumination* and *union* on the pilgrimage can easily be expounded in the context of the mountain, for the mystical teaching of St John of the Cross is shown in the image of the mountain of holiness. Evelyn Underhill spells it out:

> One of the best of all guides to these summits, St John of the Cross, drew for his disciples a picturesque map of the route. It starts straight up a very narrow path. There are two much wider and better paths going left and right; one of them is marked 'the advantages of this world' and the other 'the advantages of the next world'. Both must be avoided; for both end in the foot-hills, with no road further on. The real path goes very steeply up the mountain, to a place where St John has written, 'After this there is no path at all'; and the climber says with St Paul, 'Having nothing, I possess all things.' [1]

The Sinai texts we have before us speak of Moses' mysterious ascent of the mountain in dramatic and numinous language. The reality is as perplexing and illuminating for Moses as it is for us. A modern writer commenting on Gregory of Nyssa's *The Life of Moses* encapsulates the drama:

> In his treatise *The Life of Moses* he presented the experience of Moses climbing Mount Sinai and entering into the dark cloud of God's presence as the pattern of man's encounter with the divine. The mountain, like the desert, became an image of abandonment. There one was stripped of all egocentric concerns and transported by the stark landscape into an emptiness which only God could fill ...

According to Gregory, the soul's ascent to God involves this ascent into divine darkness. The fact that one cannot see in the dark became a powerful metaphor in Gregory's hands with which to communicate the sheer struggle and bewilderment of prayer. Prayer for Gregory was an endless longing for God, a reaching out in faith and trust for the unknowable.[2]

Gregory uses Origen's scheme of the three stages of prayer, linking them to Moses' mountain experiences:

1 The revelation of light *(phos)* at the burning bush at Horeb.
2 The obscurity of the cloud *(nephele)* in the ascent of Sinai (Exodus 19:3–6).
3 The dense, thick darkness *(gnophos)* into which God descended to speak with Moses. He calls this 'luminous darkness' beyond all knowledge and comprehension (Exodus 19:16–20).[3]

In this chapter it is helpful for us if we envisage Horeb as synonymous with Sinai. Then we can see the clear progression of Moses encountering God in light *(phos)* at the base of the mountain in the burning bush; then in cloud *(nephele)* on the higher slopes of Sinai; and lastly in the darkness *(gnophos)* on the summit.

As with the former pattern of *purgation*, *illumination* and *union*, these stages are successive and ascending. Like a spiral staircase they repeat themselves in the maturing journey of faith. When we speak of God dwelling in darkness, this is the dazzling darkness, and we experience it as such because our sight is so weak that the radiant light of God afflicts our sore eyes. The darkness into which Moses enters is that profound knowledge of God which surpasses all imagination, thought or description. The eighteenth psalm, which speaks of God bowing the heavens and descending with thick darkness under his feet (18:19), is an apt description of the divine presence enveloping Moses on Mount Sinai. This may sound strange when we recall the apostle's words: 'God is light and in him there is no darkness at all' (1 John 1:5). But we must differentiate between two kinds of darkness. As I wrote in the context of mystical prayer:

> This is a bit paradoxical because there is more than one Greek word for darkness. The New Testament word *skotos* usually has negative connotations in its metaphorical sense, but the word *gnophos* is another word for darkness which does not carry those negative meanings. It is appropriate, in John's Gospel, for Nicodemus to come to Jesus to find salvation by night, but when John says that Judas went out into the night, he means that Judas entered into the darkness of betrayal and death. It is only a seeming paradox that the time of darkness and night is often the best time for contemplative prayer in God who is light and radiance and glory and splendour. But it becomes clearer when one realizes what is happening.[4]

This language of stages or degrees of ascent is not meant to confuse the issue, or to cause the believer to become wrongly introspective about his or her spiritual life like an amateur gardener pulling up the plant to examine its root formation. It is an indication that the spiritual life is not static, but progressive, dynamic, ascending and moving on to maturity. Of course, it is also like a slippery slope down which one might slide or tumble backwards, and would therefore need to regain balance, composure and begin to ascend again.

At Horeb, Moses was confronted with the radiant knowledge of God in fire and light – an experience of both purgation and illumination. But he did not remain there. It was a kind of conversion which was meant to lead on to sanctification. He had to leave the lowland wilderness at the base of the mountain and begin to ascend. The Horeb aspect is one of light and shining knowledge experience of God, but it must lead on to the more difficult and seemingly dark and numinous terrain of sanctification – the Sinai aspect.

Believers may be children of God and servants of God, but they must progress from spiritual milk to strong food, and become disciples, friends and lovers of God. In *The Sparkling Stone,* the mystic John Ruysbroeck describes four ascending degrees of relationship with God – hirelings, faithful servants, secret friends and hidden sons.[5] We must not become obsessed with stages, steps or grades, for they vary with the writer, yet the principle of progression and move-ment holds good.

Union with God in love is the goal, and its perfection lies in the fuller life of heaven, but the pilgrim path begins at Horeb and winds on to the summit of Sinai, and beyond for those who hear the call and respond to the interior movement of the Holy Spirit.

The Obscurity of the Cloud *(nephele)*

We distinguish between the cloud *(nephele)* out of which God spoke to Moses in the first part of the chapter (19:3–6), and the dense or thick darkness *(gnophos)* into which Moses entered for mystic communion with God (19:16–20). The composite nature of the narrative text has been ordered by the later editor and it is not easy to keep track of Moses between the summit and the people, yet this simply affirms that the levels and degrees of God's manifested presence vary, run into one another, and cannot be encapsulated in water-tight compartments.

The *nephele* dimension of God speaking with Moses from the cloud was the communication of the Mosaic covenant which followed upon the Noahic and Abrahamic covenant of former days. In the covenant with Noah God's concern for all humankind is enunciated, and that though the human race deserves retribution for persistent rebellion, yet God's love is so strong that he will not allow the race to be ultimately destroyed. In the covenant with Abraham we saw the plan beginning to unfold by the choice of a particular community of people that were Abraham's seed, ultimately leading to Christ.

That community of Israel was elected to service, as a light to bring the nations to God. Israel could not become such a saving instrument until it had itself come to know the saving and redeeming power of God. This salvation experience took place in the Exodus from Egypt, with Moses leading the Israelites as prophet and saviour. What takes place on Mount Sinai is the ratification of the Exodus covenant with directions for the future journey to the promised land.

All this is happening in our narrative, as Yahweh speaks to Moses from the cloud, and Moses interprets, communicates and mediates the reality of God's word and presence on the lower slopes. God calls for an act of communal dedication. The people have been borne on eagles' wings (v. 4), they are his treasured possession (v. 5), and they are destined to become a priestly kingdom, a missionary people, holy and set apart to bring the whole earth to Yahweh in love (v. 6).

When Moses descended and brought this message to the people, they responded: 'Everything that the LORD has spoken we will do' (v. 8). This is a powerful covenant, proclaimed with light and glory, with trembling mountain and quaking people, and yet it is based on law, for the people were not ready or able to live and love spontaneously from their hearts as God yearned for them to do. This would be left until the New Covenant in Christ, when the Mosaic covenant would be superseded by the Gospel covenant, and the Holy Spirit would write God's word within the hearts of his people (2 Corinthians 3:6–11).

Throughout the New Testament it is recognized that the missionary vocation of Israel has devolved upon 'new Israel' the Church (Galatians 6:16). The Church is a 'peculiar people' (Titus 2:14), 'priests of God' (Revelation 20:6), and in

1 Peter 2:9 the themes intermingle, calling the Mosaic covenant to mind:

> You are a chosen race, a royal priesthood, a holy nation, God's own people, in order that you may proclaim the mighty acts of him who called you out of darkness into his marvellous light.

The chapters following our Exodus passage (20–34) consist of the unfolding of the commandments on the tablets of stone, leading up to the account of Moses' radiant and transfigured face (34:29–35), and the practical outworking of the instructions. The book closes with a description of the cloud of glory covering the tent of meeting and leading the people through the wilderness to the promised land. This is the same cloud that enveloped Moses on the slopes of Sinai, and which symbolizes the presence, glory and guidance of Yahweh (40:24–28).

For Gregory of Nyssa, this cloud *(nephele)* communion with God represents the second stage of Moses' journey, having moved up from the Horeb encounter with God in fire and light *(phos)*. It is followed by the third stage in which Yahweh descends in thick darkness upon the summit of the mountain, and calls Moses to ascend into the darkness *(gnophos)* of his mystery.

We have likened these stages to the classic mystical path of *purgation*, *illumination* and *union*, but most of us stay on the lower slopes of the mountain. If we have moved from purgation and into illumination, perhaps it is as much as we shall experience in this life. Even so, the pilgrimage continues into and through the veil of death, and then into a more intimate personal and corporate dimension. But for those who are haunted and impelled by the vision, and who are driven to climb towards the summit, part of that attainment may be realized in this life. This is what Gregory of Nyssa says of Moses in his restless longing to gaze upon God face to face:

Although Moses was marked out by the various great experiences of his life, he always felt somewhat unfulfilled, restless with desire. He constantly thirsted for that which had already filled him to capacity. He pleaded with God out of a sense of his own inner poverty to give him more, begging God to reveal himself to him not according to his meagre capacity to receive, but as God is in himself. What Moses was experiencing, it seems to me, was a longing which filled his soul for the supreme Good. Hope always draws the soul on from the beauty of that which is seen to that which still lies beyond; and this kindled within Moses a desire to see fully what was now hidden because only partially glimpsed. Thus, the ardent lover of beauty, although constantly the recipient of the visible images, as it were, of what he desires, always longs to be filled with the reality itself. The bold request to climb the mountains of desire is seeking to enjoy the beauty of God not in mirrors and reflections, but face to face.[6]

I am not saying that purgation and illumination are for ordinary Christians, and the unitive path is only for the elite. The way to mystical union with God in love is open to all, and ultimately all will be drawn into the ecstatic experience of unitive love in the Holy Trinity. What I am saying is that many are called but few are chosen; the calling opens up the potential, the possibility, to all – but being the kind of people we are, we do not fully respond to the God who calls us deeper into his loving mystery.

Indeed, most of us do not move far from the base of the mountain because we are content to stay there, or we are afraid of what will happen to us if we draw near to the thick darkness where God dwells. This was just the situation with the people of Israel. They witnessed the thunder and lightning, the sounding trumpet and the smoking mountain, and they were scared and trembled, and stood a long way off. They then cried out to Moses: 'You speak to us, and we will listen, but do not let God speak to us, or we will die' (20:18f.). 'Then the people stood at a distance, while Moses drew near to the thick darkness where God was' (20:21).

The writer of the Epistle to the Hebrews was saturated with the theology of Exodus, and after a powerful description of the shaking mountain and the quaking people, he says: 'Indeed so terrifying was the sight that Moses said, "I tremble with fear," ' and then he continues:

> But you have come to Mount Zion and to the city of the living God, the heavenly Jerusalem, and to innumerable angels in festal gathering, and to the assembly of the first-born who are enrolled in heaven, and to God the judge of all, and to the spirits of the righteous made perfect, and to Jesus, the mediator of a new covenant, and to the sprinkled blood that speaks a better word than the blood of Abel (11:22–24).

The Dense, Thick Darkness *(gnophos)*

I am not claiming that Moses actually entered into the highest dimension of mystical prayer which is called the unitive vision of God. What I am saying, with Gregory of Nyssa, is that these successive stages in the pilgrimage that Moses made back in the primitive days of a wild and nomadic people, *symbolize* the mystic journey.

Moses was confronted with the *vision* at Horeb at the base of the mountain; this initiated his period of ascetic *training* as he climbed upwards into the illuminative terrain of a deeper experience of God; and the call of God from the darkness enveloping the summit drew him upwards to the *achievement* of his quest and task which was to live in God, and to communicate his will. Here, the stages of the mystical path are symbolized. Moses completed the journey for his day, and we are called to complete it for ours.

We are far removed from Moses in time, and by the grace of God we have entered into the fullness of Christ's revelation and see more clearly. But the symbols of vision, struggle, darkness and achievement are still signposts on the mountain path. Lessons from Israel's history have fundamental warnings and promises which we would be wise to follow. As St Paul said: 'These things happened to them to serve as an example, and they were written to instruct us, on whom the ends of the ages have come' (1 Corinthians 10:11).

The image of the mountain is a powerful one, for this journey is a pilgrimage, and there are beautiful, verdant fields and valleys of flowers and fruits below us, breathtaking panoramic views around us in the gentle ascent, and the over-arching loveliness of spring and summer skies above us. But there are also stony, subsiding tracks leading to icy crevasses as we ascend, storms of misty fog, howling winds and blinding snow further on, with the thinning atmosphere of altitude sickness and its dizzy and perplexing consequences of disorientation and sweating fear of death.

The dense, thick darkness of Sinai into which Moses entered was no mystical picnic. The journey symbolized the high, dark mountain which St John of the Cross describes in serious, realistic language. Evelyn Underhill makes it clear:

> The word 'contemplation' easily tempts those who have not tried it to think that the mystical life consists in looking at the Everlasting Hills, and having nice feelings about God. But the world of contemplation is really continuous with the world of prayer, in the same way that the high Alps are continuous with the lower pastures. To enter it means exchanging the lovely view for the austere reality: penetrating the strange hill-country, slogging up stony tracks in heavy boots, bearing fatigue and risking fog and storm, helping fellow-climbers at one's own cost. It means renouncing the hotel-life of religion with its comforts and conveniences, and setting our face towards the snows; not for any personal ambition or enjoyment, but driven by the strange mountain love. 'Thou has made

us for Thyself and our hearts shall have no rest save in Thee.' Narrow rough paths, slippery shale, the glimpse of awful crevasses, terrible storms, cold, bewildering fog and darkness – all these wait for the genuine mountaineer. The great mystics experience all of them, and are well content so to do.[7]

Mysterium Tremendum et Fascinans

I have always been drawn to the mystical tradition, and right from the start, beginning with the lyrical mystical poetry of St John of the Cross, I realized that this was no flight of fancy, no sentimental being in tune with the Infinite, no vague and dreamy reverie in sun-blessed meadows. My study of comparative religion during theological training was deadened by university lecturers who seemed to have been touched by neither ecstasy or despair in their own experiences (with the exception of one Christian lecturer who had a Hindu wife). They seemed to illustrate the saying: 'those who study comparative religion become comparatively religious'.

But one day a book was recommended, *The Idea of the Holy*, by Rudolph Otto. First it was the title that intrigued me, but then I was bowled over by Otto's descriptive phrase: '*mysterium tremendum et fascinans*'. Words can sometimes have an hypnotic effect, of course, but *these* words carried for me an authentic ring of that which I had already discovered in my own spiritual quest.

Mysterium indicates that profound and secret glory which had hidden itself in all that is true, good and beautiful, that transcendent light which had haunted me from boyhood. *Tremendum* was that experience of awe, wonder and eerie sense of 'presence' that had often sent shivers of friendly fear and apprehension through my body, and had sometimes made the hairs on the back of my neck stand on end. *Fascinans* was that quality of spellbinding attraction that called, pulled, moved me in the depths of my spirit, and made me follow, listen, sense and touch – though not with the physical senses.

It was exactly the phrase which came into play when I read, with intuitive devotion, the 'call' passages of the prophets Isaiah (6:1–8), Jeremiah (1:4–10), Ezekiel (2:1–10) and especially in the great moments of revelation and confrontation with God which marked Moses' life, from the time when he lay in the tarred papyrus ark in the Nile (Exodus 2:3f.). I even felt about my own life that it lay beyond my birth, and I remember at some point that jump of recognition when I read the Lord's words to Jeremiah:

> Before I formed you in the womb I knew you,
> and before you were born I consecrated you … (1:5)

What was of primary importance in the life of Moses was not the content of the covenant, but the nature and character of Yahweh who gave it. For its content was a manifestation of his nature. In entering into the cloud and the darkness Moses had encountered the living God, and there had been face-to-face communion. This encounter bore the marks of a mystical meeting and indwelling in deep darkness to which all men and women of the Spirit bear witness. The following description of what John Ruysbroeck calls 'dim or dark contemplation' is the mark of the mystic who has entered into the unitive life, or as much of it as is possible on earth, and it may be read in concert with the narrative of Moses entering into the dense, thick *gnophos* darkness on Sinai:

> Here he meets God without intermediary. And from out the Divine Unity there shines into him a simple light; and this light shows him Darkness and Nakedness and Nothingness. In this Darkness he is enwrapped and falls into somewhat which is in no wise, even as one who has lost his way. In the Nakedness, he loses the perception

and discernment of all things, and is transfigured and penetrated by a simple light. In the Nothingness, all his activity fails him; for he is vanquished by the working of God's abysmal love, and in a fruitive inclination of his spirit he vanquishes God, and becomes one spirit with Him.[8]

This is a bold piece of writing from a Christian mystic, and those who are afraid of such experiential language and would like to make of the Christian faith a prophetic religion devoid of the mystical dimension feel very apprehensive of such powerful language. It is impossible to cast biblical religion into such a mould, for every prophetic encounter is shot through with mystical awareness. Indeed, if Ruysbroeck's description were to be applied to Jacob's wrestling encounter with God (Genesis 32:22–32), the mystical element would be even more obvious.

Consequences of Mystical Experience

The darkness on the summit of Sinai does not enable us to gaze, or to listen, as Moses enters into the mystery. It serves as a veil, and it is not the end of the journey for we shall see in our next chapter that Moses has yet another mountain to climb. But there are two consequences of Moses' experience on Sinai that concern us here. First, the radiance:

When Moses came down from Mount Sinai … he was not aware that his face was radiant because he had spoken with the LORD … and they were afraid to come near him (34:29–30).

The man or woman who has entered into the mystical dimension of prayer carries within an interior source of light and warmth – and sometimes this is felt or seen in the presence of such a.person, for they may radiate joy, healing or wisdom

(Acts 4:13). But sometimes it makes people afraid, as it did with the Israelites, or when Stephen's face shone like an angel's before the Sanhedrin, and they ground their teeth in fear and anger (Acts 4:13; 7:54ff.). Dwelling within the divine Presence and allowing the Holy Spirit to possess one's being manifests spiritual and physical signs of grace.

The second consequence of Moses meeting with God on Sinai is found in the last five verses of Exodus. It was that the cloud of God's continual presence and the fire of God's continual loving guidance hovered over the tabernacle and the people of God throughout the remainder of their pilgrim journey:

> For the cloud of the LORD was on the tabernacle by day, and the fire was in the cloud by night, before the eyes of all the house of Israel at each stage of their journey (40:34–48).

Prayer

Lord God of fire, cloud and darkness: You called from the mountain to your servant Moses, and filled him with spiritual wisdom and prophetic power.

Grant me, I pray, a vision of your glory; take me deeper into the wonders of your love; strengthen me to enter the deep darkness of your secret ways.

In all your dealings with my soul, let me reflect your radiance. Amen.

*

Action

Look back over the stages of your life, and write down some of the significant experiences (from within or from circumstances) that have moved you with joy or fear.

Reflect upon them and ask if they may have a bearing upon your present thinking or future action. After honestly writing up these experiences, take them to a trusted priest, pastor or friend and leave them with him/her for a short period. Then meet up to talk over the material.

From the outset expect that something positive will come of this exercise, and be prepared to act accordingly.

5

Mount Nebo

Viewing the Promised Land:
Deuteronomy 34:1–12

Then Moses went up from the plains of Moab to Mount Nebo, to the top of Pisgah, which is opposite Jericho, and the LORD showed him the whole land ... the LORD said to him, 'This is the land of which I swore to Abraham, to Isaac, and to Jacob, saying, "I will give it to your descendants"; I have let you see it with your eyes, but you shall not cross over there.' Then Moses, the servant of the LORD died there in the land of Moab, at the LORD's command. Moses was one hundred and twenty years old when he died; his sight was unimpaired and his vigour had not abated.

Unanswered Prayer

One would have thought that having faced the rigours of Sinai with its thunder and lightning, its smoke and fire, the unearthly sounding of the trumpet and the fearful entry into the thick darkness of the presence of Yahweh, Moses would have been ready for anything. But there was another mountain, another strange climb, and a summit experience that was, at the same time, the near fulfilment of all his hopes and expectations, and the saddest moment of his long life.

The mountain was Nebo (also called Pisgah), rising over 2,600 feet above the Plain of Moab, north-east of the Dead Sea. From its summit the Jordan river flowed below and stretching westwards towards the Mediterranean Sea was the whole land of Canaan – the Promised Land. This summit should have been the highest peak in Moses' life, the exhilarating consummation of all his hopes and plans, the reward for all his dedication, toil and tears. But it didn't quite work out like that.

There are three Deuteronomic passages which witness to Moses' Nebo experience. They look like this:

1 3:23–29: Moses is forbidden to cross the Jordan.
2 32:8–52: Moses is to view the land 'only from a distance', and to prepare for his death.
3 34:1–12: Moses' death and eulogy.

Let's look at the first passage. Moses realizes that the long trek is almost over. He has led the people to the border of the Promised Land – it only means crossing over the river Jordan and entering into his inheritance. You can almost hear the singing

> Swing low, sweet chariot,
> Coming for to carry me home ...

in the stanza from that beautiful Negro Spiritual which speaks of looking over Jordan and seeing the ministering angels winging their way. But there is anbiguity here – for the river of Jordan is not only the beginning of a new life, but it is the river of death.

Moses falls down before the Lord in a prayer that encapsulates all his hopes and dreams. He reminds God of all that his power and wisdom have accomplished up to this moment, and calls upon him to consummate the work and to bring to fulfilment all his deepest hopes and aspirations: 'Let me go over and see the good land beyond the Jordan ...' And the Lord says 'No!'

I remember being told as a child: 'When you pray for something really important, remember there are three possible answers: 'Yes! No! Wait!' Moses had been waiting ... waiting, and his age is now calculated at three generations (3 × 40 years). The moment has come, and his prayer ascends in hope and faith. And the answer is No! As clear, as firm and as adamant as that. We puzzle about unanswered prayer because we are not willing to receive the answer which is at hand. And for that reason we fail to hear what is being said on the other side of the negative answer.

Moses had no option, for he felt the anger and judgement of the Lord, and as he relates this experience to the people, he adds these significant words ... 'Because of you the LORD was angry with me and would not listen to me' (3:26).

Vicarious Suffering

There is something strange here, for we shall see in the second passage that together with Aaron, Moses acted impatiently at Meribah in striking the rock for water, because of the people's rebellion (32:5of.). But here he is saying that he is bearing the Lord's anger and judgement on the people's account. He was reiterating something he had already told them about unbelievers not entering the land of promise: 'Because of you the LORD became angry with me also and said, "You shall not enter it" ' (1:37).

Here is an instance of the prophet 'standing for the people' and entering into the suffering, and even the pain, involved It has been called 'corporate personality', and means that one man can stand for the people as representative, and they can be summed or headed up in him. There is a solidarity of the race in Adam, a solidarity of the faithful in Abraham. In the great prophetic ministry of leaders like Isaiah, Jeremiah and Ezekiel, the prophets groaned, wept and interceded for the people in their own persons. This was particularly so in the case of Moses, for he stood before God as mediator and intercessor.

There is a certain vicariousness in *representing* the people, and a willingness to bear not only their pain and suffering, but also their judgement. See how it works in the ministry of Moses, of the apostle Paul, and supremely and uniquely in Christ himself:

1 'Alas, this people has sinned a great sin; ... But now, if you will only forgive their sin – but if not, blot me out of the book that you have written' (32:31f.).
2 'I could wish that I myself were accursed and cut off from Christ for the sake of my own people, my kindred according to the flesh' (Romans 9:3).
3 'He saved others; he cannot save himself' (Mark 15:31).

If there was a sense in which Moses was under the judgement of God on account of the people's sin, and he was forbidden to enter the land of promise because of them, this only serves as a pointer to Christ. Speaking of the suffering of Christ before the Sanhedrin, the apostle Peter quoted Moses from Deuteronomy 18:15:

> Moses said, 'The Lord your God will raise up for you from your own people a prophet like me. You must listen to whatever he tells you' (Acts 3:22, see also 7:37).

When Paul identifies himself closely with the people of God in his prophetic and priestly ministry, he makes this daring statement:

> I am now rejoicing in my sufferings for your sake, and in my flesh I am completing what is lacking in Christ's afflictions for the sake of his body, that is the church (Colossians 1:24).

Neither Moses nor Paul could 'bear the sins' of God's people in a redemptive sense, of course, but they were representatives in that they entered most profoundly and intimately into the sufferings and sins of the people. Christ alone was the great sin-bearer, the paschal lamb who 'bore away the sins of the world', but Moses points forward to the Suffering Servant, and Paul looks back to the crucified Saviour, and both of them share in Christ's redemptive sufferings as far as they were able.

Moses' Crowning Joy

The Bible is realistic in that it does not round off the story with Moses receiving the reward of all his life's toil and labour. His most urgent longing is refused, and he has to learn that he has accomplished that which God had in mind for him, and pray, not in resignation, but in obedient acceptance: 'Your will be done.'

In other words, his crowning joy is to receive from God's hand that perfect will, in acceptance of which is Moses' peace. That is, to climb up to the top of Mount Nebo, look north, south, east and west in the evaluation of his life's ministry, to hand over his charism, blessing and encouragement to Joshua, and accept the good and gentle death which God has ordained for him below the slopes of the mountain.

There is a certain joy, and often a relief, in the acceptance of something which you intuitively felt was God's will for you. A spirit of trust and acceptance is the mark of God's Holy Spirit within. Suppose today you realized that you had to stop struggling and fighting, and simply learn to live with your increasing physical limitations? Suppose, after prayer and counsel, you came to the conclusion that your life's hopes, ambitions and carefully planned life's work were not the will of God? Could you accept that in good grace, leaving the consequences in God's hands? Or suppose you heard your doctor's diagnosis of terminal illness, and a prognosis of six months or one year to live? Could you receive that positively, and prepare for a good, worthy and gentle death?

I have the *Order of Service* of the Thanksgiving Service for the life of Donald Nicholl, that saintly Roman Catholic layman. It contains some of the reflections of his friends, among which is this from Fr Roderick Strange:

> When I heard that he was ill, I telephoned him and he told me simply and directly that he was preparing himself for death, which he described as a serious task. 'I must give it my proper attention,' he said, 'so that it is in harmony with what I believe and the way I have tried to live.' And he directed me to Colossians 1:24, which he explained gave him great comfort. 'Now I rejoice in my sufferings for your sake, and in my flesh I complete what is lacking in Christ's afflictions for the sake of his body, the church.' And Donald died in such acceptance, and is remembered with great joy.

Now none of us is expected to leap with joyful and positive response to the questions raised above. But if the time came, if the questions were asked, then it would be time for us to turn in our need to God, remembering his former faithfulness, and trust him for living or dying grace. This need not be second best, but the blessed will of God.

Viewing from a Distance

Turning to the second Deuteronomic passage (32:48–52), this is a repetition of what we have already noted, with an emphasis upon viewing the Promised Land from a distance. Things look so much different when you step back, walk away, climb a mountain and take a long, thoughtful, mature and objective look at your life and situation.

I remember one of our novices coming to me and saying that he felt the immersion in the extremely busy life of our mother house was pressurizing him and causing such stress that he could not live or pray in any contentment. He needed the time and space to test his vocation, and although it is a testing time, and a certain amount of stress is good and necessary for us, in his case it was counterproductive.

So I told him to climb the hill behind the friary, bearing in mind the word 'perspective'. From the top, on a clear day, he would see three counties, and from that vantage point he would be able to evaluate not only the busy life of the friary, but also his own life in the light of eternity. It did the trick – he returned with a new spring in his step. I guess that whenever he was busily involved with his work in the friary after that, his heart would rise to the top of Batcombe Down.

Whenever I read any of the Mount Nebo accounts, I cannot help seeing the figure of Moses gazing out over the river Jordan into the land of promise from the vantage point of the hymn writer Isaac Watts. It isn't quite fair to Moses, though, for there is no indication that he was looking over the river of death, and by faith viewing the heavenly Canaan beyond his immediate mortal life as Watts makes out in his hymn 'There is a Land of Pure Delight'.[1]

We must accept Moses' story as it stands and affirm that faith is good enough for this life alone, and were there 'no heaven to gain and no hell to shun' we would still be content, even enthusiastic in following the gospel path for love's sake. And we would! But we do not live in the dim understanding of the Deuteronomist who had no developed sense that the kingdom of God is everlasting, or that one can gaze out and beyond our finitude and mortality into the larger life beyond the death of the body. We accept Moses' perspective, and believe that God was not teasing or being nasty to him, but enabling him to accept positively that his task was done, that Joshua would carry on the work, and that he must now offer his life to God in death.

Nevertheless, we are Easter people, and so there is every reason for us to take this symbol of Moses climbing, waiting and gazing over into the promised Canaan, and to sing Watts's hymn at the end of the chapter.

Dying and the Will of God

Our third Deuteronomic passage concludes the book, and both the mountain's names are found in the first verse. Perhaps we can think of Nebo as the aspect of dying, and Pisgah as the aspect of faith's contemplation. By doing this we shall be able to take our own death seriously, while realizing that the Lord who stands beside us on the summit of the mountain is the One who will carry us into the kingdom of his love when our earthly pilgrimage is over. It is not infrequent to find mountaineers speaking of 'a presence' that accompanied or helped them in moments of crisis or loneliness on the long slog. Frank Smythe tells this story of his Everest climb:

All the time that I was climbing alone I had a strong feeling that I was accompanied by a second person. This feeling was so strong that it completely eliminated all loneliness I might otherwise have felt. It even seemed that I was tied to my 'companion' by a rope, and that if I slipped 'he' would hold me. I remember constantly glancing back over my shoulder, and once, when after reaching my highest point, I stopped to try and eat some mint cake, I carefully divided it and turned round with one half in my hand. It was almost a shock to find no one to whom to give it. It seemed to me that this 'presence' was a strong, helpful and friendly one, and it was not until Camp VI was sighted that the link connecting me, as it seemed at the time, to the beyond was snapped, and although Shipton and the camp were but a few yards away, I suddenly felt alone.[2]

When Peter Habeler and Reinhold Messner successfully climbed Everest in May 1978 they entered into severe life-threatening conditions, such as a 200-kms-an-hour raging wind. With physical reserves exhausted towards the top they could scarcely take ten paces at a time. At over 8,700 metres altitude, concentration had deteriorated and, battered by the wind, Habeler dragged himself up the final section of the Summit Ridge.

At this point he prayed: 'Lord God, let me go right to the top. Give me the power to remain alive, don't let me die up here.' He crawled on elbows and knees, praying fervently and felt he was in dialogue with a higher being and being pushed to the heights. 'And suddenly I was up again on my own two feet: I was standing on the summit.' [3]

His request was granted. Moses' request was not. But even in the refusal, God had a better way, for to die in the will of God is better than to live outside it. Moses had dim perceptions of the other side of death. At best it was being 'gathered to his fathers' in a hazy underworld of half-consciousness called *Sheol*. But the reality was beyond his wildest Canaan dreams. He had another appointment on another mountain. That mountain was Tabor, and the appointment was with the Messiah!

The Greatness of Moses

Eulogies are strange things. They sometimes make you think that you are at the funeral of a different person to the one whose name is on the coffin. Obituaries are getting better because they are more honest than they used to be. In our own *Society of St Francis* one had to read between the lines to find out what was being said in the obituary of a brother or sister. But now it is possible to read and hear, for example, that Brother Jeremiah was an awkward old cuss, with a bad temper, too hearty an appetite and a powerful dislike of chapter meetings – but also a man of integrity!

The Bible does not hide the faults of Moses – his early cowardice, evasions, excuses, impatience and disobedience. But here, at the conclusion of the book and at the end of his life there is a marvellous write-up of what he had accomplished.

Even more than Abraham or Jacob, he found a nation in bondage and led them into liberty. Almost alone he took a stubborn, rebellious band of tribes related by religion and blood, and made them into a nation for God. With fiery zeal and loving compassion he communicated humility and dedication, and in the middle of an arid and inhospitable desert his courage and confidence in Yahweh caused the people of Israel to develop a trust and an endeavour that they could never have achieved alone.

I am just in the middle of listening to a sermon preached by Martin Luther King at Mount Zion Church, Cincinnati, Ohio, called 'A Knock at Midnight', which was sent to me by a gentle Quaker. It is not one of his great sermons, but here and now, over 30 years on, it communicates power, humour, discerning perception and prophetic dynamic. He is angry with an amazing humility, and the people are playfully enjoying his description of their 'enemies' at one moment, and reduced to trembling awe and wonder at his denunciation of their sins at another.

We can now look at Martin Luther King from this distance and know him to be a man of integrity, of honesty, justice and reconciliation. It comes through on the recording, for 'he being dead yet speaks', and it comes through in all the circumstances and accomplishments that are the summation of his life and martyrdom. He was a black Moses, and it seems to me a wonderful synchronicity that the words and passion of such a man should sound in my hermitage as I am praying and writing about the stature of Moses.

Another comparison comes to me when I read that 'Moses was 120 years old when he died: his eye was not dim, nor his natural force abated'. The unique Hebrew word for *natural force* has to do with the moist freshness of sap, and indicates virility, charism and both physical and mental prowess. In the two other places it occurs (outside the Bible in Ugaritic texts), its meaning is *life-force* in opposition to human weakness in sickness and death.

My second comparison is with Antony, the prototype of the Christian hermit. He was born about AD 251 and retreated into the Egyptian desert at 20 years of age after hearing the words of Jesus in church: 'If you wish to be perfect, go, sell your possessions and give the money to the poor ... then come, follow me' (Matthew 19:21). The story goes that over 20 years later his friends broke into his solitary hermitage and found that physically he had not deteriorated by his ascetic training, but had improved; he was not fat through lack of exercise, or dried up from fasting and fighting the powers of darkness. Physically and mentally he is described as 'all balanced, as one governed by reason and standing in his natural condition'.[4]

Unlike pagan dualism, which is ashamed of the body, Antony's state is contrasted right up to his death when he was still sound in all his senses and vigorous in all his limbs. Even his teeth were all there, though worn down to the gums – at about 105 years of age! Even allowing for a bit of exaggeration on the part of Deuteronomy and Athanasius – the authors – something remarkable is being said about Antony and Moses.

The time has come for us to leave Mount Nebo, and to allow the mystery of God's burial of Moses to take place hidden from human sight. But bearing in mind the evaluation of the final three verses, we may say that there has been no prophet like Moses in the story of Israel, whom the Lord knew face to face, for he was a charismatic leader, priest, ruler, judge and saviour of his people, and as prophet laid the foundation of what the later eighth-century prophets taught about the nature and character of Yahweh. Let his be our last word as he points to the future Messiah: 'The LORD your

God will raise up for you a prophet like me from among your
own people; you shall heed such a prophet' (Deuteronomy
18:15).

Prayer

> There is a land of pure delight,
>   Where saints immortal reign;
> Infinite day excludes the night,
>   And pleasures banish pain.
>
> Sweet fields beyond the swelling flood
>   Stand dressed in living green;
> So to the Jews old Canaan stood,
>   While Jordan rolled between.
>
> Could we but climb where Moses stood,
>   And view the landscape o'er,
> Not Jordan's stream, nor death's cold flood,
>   Should fright us from the shore! [5]

*

Action

I want to suggest that you climb your own Nebo. Take a walk
into your local cemetery and look at the epitaphs. Think
about those people and what we have said about Moses.

Then write a 'one line' epitaph and then a 'considered'
epitaph on your own life – not what you would like it to be,
but what it *would* be, from the inside. Be honest! Reflect upon
it, either by laying it before God in prayer or by using it as the
basis of confession with priest, pastor or friend.

The assumption is that it will give you discernment and
knowledge of what has been, and a hopeful new direction for
the rest of your life.

6

Mount Carmel

Consuming Fire: 1 Kings 18:16–39

At the time of the offering of the oblation, the prophet Elijah came near and said, 'O LORD, God of Abraham, Isaac and Israel, let it be known that you are God in Israel, that I am your servant, and that I have done all these things at your bidding. Answer me, O LORD, answer me, so that this people may know that you, O LORD, are God, and that you have turned their hearts back.' Then the fire of the LORD fell and consumed the burnt-offering, the wood, the stones, and the dust, and even licked up the water that was in the trench. When all the people saw it, they fell on their faces and said, 'The LORD, indeed is God; the LORD indeed is God.'

Valour and Cowardice

From my twelfth year I used to participate in the annual Sunday School Union scripture examinations. I remember clearly the year in which we studied the cycle of Elijah stories. From the opening text I was smitten:

Now Elijah the Tishbite, of Tishbe in Gilead, said to Ahab, 'As the LORD the God of Israel lives, before whom I stand, there shall be neither dew nor rain these years, except by my word' (1 Kings 17:1).

This was the great Elijah confronting the wicked Ahab, and he strode across the chapters of the Old Testament as a mighty prophet, a new Moses, the scourge of evil and hypocrisy, calling back idolatrous Israel to the worship of Yahweh the true God.

Not only was he a mighty preacher and reformer, but he was accompanied by the power of God. When we got to the fire and passion of Mount Carmel in my reading, I expressed my boyhood admiration in song, as I yearned to be possessed of the same fiery zeal:

> God of Elijah, hear our cry:
>   Send the fire!
> And make us fit to live or die:
>   Send the fire!
> Oh, see us on Your altar lay
> Our lives, our all this very day;
> To crown the offering now, we pray:
>   Send the fire!

So I was a little perplexed when I discovered, immediately following the contest on Mount Carmel, and the miraculous restoration of rain, that as soon as Elijah heard of the anger of the heathen Queen Jezebel, he got scared for his life, ran down to Beersheba and fell into a deep depression (1 Kings 19:1–6).

One of the lessons I had to learn, even at that age, was that the solitary man may also be a lonely man, that the man mighty in valour may also be a coward, and that the man on whose word lay the issues of life and death may also be 'a man of like passions' as ourselves (James 5:17).

Even as a boy, going through these ancient texts in the King James version, I began to see clearly that however ruggedly individual a man like Elijah might be, standing before all the power and dangers of a heathen monarchy and idolatrous people, he also had his vulnerable spots. He could sink down into an inconsolable melancholy when left to himself. The natural gifts must be consecrated to God, and the natural fears and weaknesses must be acknowledged and confessed to God. Only on such a basis could a man or woman respond to the prophetic vocation and fulfil the otherwise impossible task that God lays upon the prophetic soul.

The Lonely Mountain Climber

When the German mountaineer Reinhold Messner reflected upon the loneliness of his mountain vocation following his solo climb of the 8,000-metre Nanga Parbat mountain in the Karakoram in 1973, he spoke of his physical strength and psychological weakness. Like Elijah, he realized the difference between solitude and loneliness: that being alone on a mountain doesn't guarantee an experience of utter loneliness, and that mingling in a crowd need not deprive you of true solitude.

By 1980 he had grown in self-awareness and humility, and in a solo ascent of Everest without oxygen, he reflected on the failure and death of Mallory and Irvine in 1924 at the point where they were both lost. His own reflections are worth contemplating as we imagine the preparation and inward life of Elijah faced with the mammoth task of single-handedly bringing the people of Israel back to Yahweh. Messner writes:

> As I lose my orientation success is far from my mind. I'm thinking for the moment. The psychological burden of searching a way through the rock, clouds and ice up to the couloir, then a steep snow flank leading on to the rocky buttress extending down from the Summit Pyramid, weighs heavily on my spirit. Can I carry it? ... While sitting on top of Nanga in '78 I felt as though I was born again, a witness to the whole creation. Now I've brought another dream into reality but there are no words to express this

new feeling. The physical stress has reached its limit and the mind can't even react during that instant. I'm simply there. At times I've searched out a face-to-face encounter with loneliness that was no longer a handicap but a strength. But in no way could I ever claim to have found aloneness. I've merely opened a few doors. Slowly and carefully, step by step, I've learned to know something of myself, to love myself. Sometimes I took chances, I dared, and other times I held back too long. But along my way there's no turning back. I'm delighted on my voyage inward, for there is always room to grow.[1]

This is not simply a physical and psychological journey that Messner is making; he is probing into areas of spirituality in his interior mountain ascent. He speaks of a quest of the spirit as he finds and loses orientation; a self-question as to his ability to carry it through; a sense of new birth into a cosmic awareness with its accompanying ineffability. He breaks through from simple loneliness into something approaching solitude, but falls short of his yearning, and in the process comes to know himself more clearly and love himself more dearly.

Chancing and daring are part of the adventure, and some-times there is the fear of really letting go, but having gone thus far there is no return. It has become an inward voyage with infinite room for growth and maturity.

It may seem a strange exercise to link Messner and Elijah as lonely mountain climbers, but there are parallels in their inward journey that are common to all who venture on to the ascending mountain. After St John of the Cross escaped from his prison he spent a few months in the foothills of the Segura mountains. Every week he went to minister to the sisters in Beas, a journey of five or six miles. If one looks at the route it means either a meandering long way which takes hours, or a more direct route which involves climbing. The latter is presumably the way he went. Between journeys John sketched cards for the sisters on which he drew his famous mountain with wide paths on either side leading to dead ends, and one straight, narrow, direct path to the summit leading to the broad, spacious summit of the vision of God.

This is the direct path that Elijah took in all his boldness and vulnerability, and this is the way we are invited and challenged to follow – in our own way and according to our own time, within the will of God.

Elijah, Reinhold Messner and St John of the Cross – all loners describing solo climbs, solitary paths, interior journeys of self-awareness and confrontation, learning to know oneself and to love oneself in the process. But although the journey has to be personal, it is not meant to be individualistic, and there is often the joy of a partner, a group or a whole company of people sharing the way. The lonely prophet in the Old Testament, the retreat and Arabia patterns of the New Testament, the hermit tradition of the desert – all these, including ourselves, follow the pattern of the lonely Jesus, who blazed the trail for others to follow, and who pioneered alone in order that he might bring many children to glory (Hebrews 2:10).

People may be *lost* alone, for sin and rebellion breaks unity into fragments, but no one is *saved* alone. Men and women are 'saved into' a fellowship, and that fellowship is the people of God. There may be many experiences of loneliness, isolation and suffering on the journey, but in both suffering and pilgrimage the traveller is still in the company of fellow-travellers on earth, and surrounded by the communion of saints above. Whether the image is the mountain path or the athlete's race, the truth is the same:

Therefore, since we are surrounded by so great a cloud of witnesses, let us also lay aside every weight and the sin that clings so closely, and let us run with perseverence the race that is set before us, looking to Jesus the pioneer and perfecter of our faith (Hebrews 12:1f.).

Elijah was not alone, though he did not know it (18:4; 19:18), but before we look at the Carmel episode more closely, see what Thomas Merton writes about the mountain path:

> The journey without maps leads him into rugged moun-
> tainous country where there are often mists and storms
> and where he is more and more alone. Yet at the same time,
> ascending the slopes in darkness, feeling more and more
> keenly his own emptiness, and with the winter wind
> blowing through his now tattered garments, he meets at
> times other travellers on the way, poor pilgrims as he is,
> and as solitary as he, belonging perhaps to other lands and
> other traditions. There are, of course, great differences
> between them, and yet they have much in common.[2]

Preparations for Mount Carmel

After the death of King Solomon, his kingdom was split into two parts. The south under Rehoboam his son, and the north under Jeroboam, 'who made Israel to sin'. In order to stop people going south to worship at Jerusalem, Jeroboam set up two temples at Dan and Bethel, and in each he placed a golden calf, so that the God of Israel might be worshipped under such a form (1 Kings 12:28). Eventually, after much military expeditions and bloodshed, the kingdom passed into the hands of a political strategist, Omri, who was an especially wicked sovereign, and then to his son, Ahab, 'who did evil in the sight of the Lord more than all who were before him' (16:30).

Ahab's accession is dated about 870 BC, and his marriage to Jezebel, princess of Tyre, brought out the worst in him, and he became the tool of a crafty, unscrupulous and cruel woman.

She sought to eliminate the worship of Yahweh and turn the nation from the Mosaic tradition to the worship of Baal. The Baals were the local heathen fertility gods set up at every village shrine, and they were all local manifestations of the great sky-god Baal who controlled weather and fertility.

A temple was built to the goddess Astarte near Jezreel and a huge temple for Baal in Samaria, the capital of the northern kingdom. Heathen shrines and altars multiplied, the prophets of Yahweh were hunted and slain, and the altars of Yahweh, like the one on Mount Carmel, were desecrated and abandoned. There was a small, faithful remnant, like the group hidden in the limestone caves of Carmel by the pious Obadiah (18:3f.), but due to the influence of Ahab and Jezebel, the northern kingdom became largely heathen.

Tishbe, in Gilead, lay east of the Jordan, and its inhabitants were, like its terrain, wild, unkempt and rough. Elijah grew up among such people, physically rugged and sinewy and well able to outrun the softer people of the lowlands.

Because of its geographical situation in the mountainous desert country, the Yahweh tradition was still relatively unaffected by the insidious teaching of Jezebel's prophets. As Elijah grew into manhood he became increasingly zealous for the Yahweh tradition, especially when travellers told of the massacre of God's prophets and their replacement by the Tyrian deities and idolatry.

This stirred up Elijah's indignation, and he remembered the denunciation made by Moses years before that if they turned aside from serving the living God the heavens would be shut up with consequent drought and famine because of disobedience and idolatry (Deuteronomy 11:17). So the first thing that Elijah did was to fall on his face before God in prayer (James 5:17).

At some point along the way there was a prophetic call which shook Elijah to his depths, as it always did in the prophetic tradition, and after chapters of wickedness and apostasy in the first book of Kings, there bursts upon the scene this wild prophet with a commission from Yahweh. So we come to the dramatic text which caught my attention as a twelve-year-old boy:

Now Elijah the Tishbite, of Tishbe in Gilead, said to Ahab, 'As the LORD the God of Israel lives, before whom I stand, there shall be neither dew nor rain these years, except by my word' (17:1).

Then he disappeared!

While Elijah is hidden from the view of Ahab and Jezebel, who certainly would have killed him, we see him drawn by the word of the Lord for three years of silence and solitude into the ravine of Cherith, sustained by the ravens' morning and evening bread and by the long-lasting stream of the wadi.

Then the drought took hold, the wadi dried up, and he found hospitality and a testing of his charismatic powers at the house of the widow of Zarephath in Sidon (17:2–4).

Then he reappeared!

We have noted the two words for *time* in the New Testament – *chronos* and *kairos*. *Chronos* is clock time and the three years of retreat and learning that Elijah spent at Cherith and Zarephath were *chronos* years. *Kairos* is the moment of opportunity and maturity, when 'the time is fulfilled' (Mark 1:15). God leads us out of a busy and frenetic public life into solitude and prayer for our preparation, and when the time is right he thrusts us forth into a place of prophetic ministry. That is what he did with Elijah.

I have an icon of Elijah the Prophet before me as I write. He is sitting pensively by the Wadi Cherith, gazing upwards at the large, black raven who flies in with a large circular piece of bread in its beak. This is preparation for Carmel, and is a wonderful indication that there can be no Carmel without Cherith, and no Spirit-filled confrontation or divine fire without the quiet place of contemplation and prayer.

We all experience this in different ways: when, in obedience to God's leading, I took off with my caravan in 1990 to the enclosure of the plum orchard on the grounds of Tymawr Convent some miles from Monmouth, it was my Cherith.

I was there in basic solitude for three years, and in the

homily I preached for the nuns at my farewell eucharist, I told them that I felt like the prophet Elijah who had spent his three years at Cherith – there was a stream at the bottom of the fields running down to Redbrook. I told them that one commentator thought that the 'ravens' were a community of wandering nomads who sustained Elijah, and therefore I felt that this homily might be the reflections of the departing Elijah to the group of ravens in their habits! They appreciated the analogy, and I was able to express something of my appreciation and joy for their loving and silent hospitality during that time of preparation. But the time had come to move!

On to the Mountain

King Ahab and servant Obadiah had been searching for water to preserve the remaining cattle in the terrible drought. Suddenly Obadiah found Elijah towering over him, and fell down, scared and trembling. The exchange was brief and to the point, and soon Ahab appeared with the words: 'Is it you, you troubler of Israel?' Elijah threw the accusation back in his face, and yet Ahab was right – Elijah *was* troubling Israel with a prophetic power because of the people's apostasy and idolatry. The true prophet is not meant to comfort the afflicted but to afflict the comfortable! Elijah then issued an imperative:

> Now therefore have all Israel assemble for me at Mount Carmel, with the four hundred and fifty prophets of Baal and the four hundred prophets of Asherah, who eat at Jezebel's table (18:19).

The scene is set. It is early morning on Mount Carmel. All work has been abandoned and crowds of Israelites have assembled at this sacred place, just below the summit where the scattered stones of the desecrated altar of Yahweh lie around. Ahab has summoned people and prophets. The 450 prophets of Baal are present, bearing the emblems of their fertility god, with Ahab in his royal litter.

Jezebel is absent; likewise are her 400 Astarte prophets. Has she countermanded the king's decree? Is she afraid, or is she defiant? The question is in the air, but there is also a profound stirring of trembling and yearning in the hearts of the people. Something wonderful or fearful is about to happen, and the air is thick with the presence of mystery. It is almost too much to bear, but the people are spellbound and cannot move. Rudolph Otto's phrase is applicable: *Mysterium tremendum et fascinans.*

In spite of the overwhelming Baalite priestly majority, Elijah takes the initiative, and preparations are obviously in hand. There are seven moments of intervention in the proceedings as he, filled with prophetic fervour and assurance, leads the way. Let's follow them:

1. The Question: 'How long will you go limping with two different opinions?' (18:21). The Hebrew term means hopping from one leg to another, and Elijah is making it clear that no one can serve two masters – it is either Baal or Yahweh! He goes on: 'If the LORD is God, follow him; but if Baal, then follow him.' The people are speechless.

2. The Challenge: Elijah declares his minority – with God! – and he proposes the pattern of the challenge. Two bulls are to be prepared, laid on the wood on a stone altar, and prayer is to be offered for fire from heaven. And the outcome? '… the god who answers by fire is indeed God' (18:24). And everyone agrees.

3. The Rebuke: There is a moment of relief as action is anticipated, and the priests of Baal prepare and lay the bull on their altar, relying on the belief that Baal the fertility god rules the elements and can send fire and restore the rain.

So when everything is in order they begin their heathen liturgy – there is chanting, dancing, crying, wailing, leaping and frenzy – and this continues for three hours. However, not one spark is ignited. At noon Elijah shouts above the pandemonium his words of rebuke, and they have in them the sting of sarcasm: 'Cry aloud! Surely he is a god; either he is meditating or he has wandered away, or he is on a journey, or perhaps he is asleep and must be awakened' (18:27).

Noon is the zenith of Baal's sun-god power, and the priests redouble their efforts, cry out in trance and hysterically cut and mutilate themselves drawing forth blood. But there is no answer – the altar is cold and the offering smokeless. This continues until the time of the evening oblation in the distant temple of Yahweh in Jerusalem, and then Elijah intervenes.

4. The Invitation: 'Come closer to me,' calls Elijah, and the people encircle him. He acts quietly, deliberately and in parable. First he repairs the desecrated Yahweh altar, taking twelve stones, indicating the election and unity of the twelve tribes of the one Israel. When it is complete he dedicates it in the name of Yahweh. Then he digs a trench all around, sets the wood in order, and lays the prepared bull on the wood – all in silence. Then he speaks.

5. The Command: 'Fill four jars with water and pour it on the offering and on the wood.' They do it. And again. And again. And the water saturates the offering, wood, altar and runs into the trench. There is no possibility of a secret spark or pseudo-flame.

6. The Invocation: Elijah waits for the time of the evening oblation, then in concert with the offering in the temple of Yahweh, he steps forward, raises his hands and prays clearly, calling on the name of Yahweh.

Then the fire falls!

There is consternation, for the flame descends, consuming the sacrifice, burning up the wood, blackening the stones, scattering the ashes and even licking up the water in the trench. The people gaze, open-mouthed with wonder, then fall on their faces and cry out: 'Yahweh indeed is God; Yahweh indeed is God.'

7. The Judgement: Elijah points to the prophets of Baal and condemns them. They are hastened to the Wadi Kishon further down Mount Carmel and executed. Then Elijah tells Ahab that there is the sound of rushing rain in his ears, and he climbs to the top of Carmel to pray.

It was all very dramatic, and though there was a long and quiet preparation, when the moment of confrontation on Carmel came, it was deadly serious – the lordship of Baal or the lordship of Yahweh – and there is a world of difference!

But now for Elijah the time of intercession has come and we must leave him to the conclusion of this amazing day and the torrent of rain which is evident in the banking clouds of the sky.

This is not the end for him – for Carmel was but one mountain and one experience in his long ministry. Disillusion, depression, renewal and transcendent vision await him until that day when the fiery chariot and horses of Yahweh carry him to his reward in the sight of his successor, Elisha.

But our story is over, and our Mount Carmel has to be climbed. It may not be as dramatic or as sanguine, but it will require serious preparation and the faith and courage that God alone can give.

I think back to those boyhood days with which I began this chapter, and remember another stanza of that old hymn, combining the fire of Elijah with the fire of Pentecost:

To make our weak hearts strong and brave:
    Send the fire!
To live a dying world to save:
    Send the fire!
Look down and see this waiting host,
Give us the promised Holy Ghost,
We want another Pentecost:
    Send the fire!

Prayer

God of fire and judgement:

   *Prepare my heart for the coming of your Holy Spirit; lead
me into the solitude where I am sustained by the bread of life
and the water of your word;*

   *Make me ready to receive the fire and flame of Carmel,
and help me to bear it;*

   *Grant that I may follow you with an undivided heart.
Amen.*

*

Action:

Consider what spiritual drought means in your life
                        – write it down!
Consider what the fire of God means in your life
                        – write it down!
Consider what torrential rain means in your life
                        – write it down!
Consider the difference all these could make
                           – live it out!

Mount Tabor

Transfiguring Light: Matthew 17:1–9

*Jesus took with him Peter and James and his brother John
and led them up a high mountain, by themselves. And he
was transfigured before them, and his face shone like the
sun, and his clothes became dazzling white. Suddenly there
appeared to them Moses and Elijah talking with him. Then
Peter said to Jesus, 'Lord, it is good for us to be here; if you
wish, I will make three dwellings here, one for you, one for
Moses, and one for Elijah.' While he was still speaking,
suddenly a bright cloud overshadowed them, and from the
cloud a voice said, 'This is my Son, the Beloved; with him I
am well pleased; listen to him!' When the disciples heard
this, they fell to the ground and were overcome by fear. But
Jesus came and touched them, saying, 'Get up and do not
be afraid.' And when they looked up, they saw no one
except Jesus himself alone.*

Suffering and Glory

We have accompanied Moses who entered the darkness and
light of Sinai's glory, and Elijah whose prophetic word and
prayer called down the divine fire on Mount Carmel. These
two men represent the root and flower of Israel, who by their
lives and words show us that suffering is the way to glory.
They are the bearers of the covenant of law and obedience,

but glorious as that covenant was, it was temporal. These were men of passion and prophecy, but they caught only glimpses of the divine mystery. What they saw, they saw with courage and penetration, but they needed to be encouraged and sustained each step of the way. They fell on their faces before the wonder of God, but if he had revealed himself in the fullness of the divine Love they would have perished under the burden, the vision and the supernatural light.

Their stature, as the two great prophets, is in no way diminished for their own day. Moses was the prototype and Elijah the forerunner, but now we come to the eternal sun at its full zenith. Moses and Elijah have truly led us along the path of revelation, but now, with them we turn our eyes to the One who entered into the world's suffering, and bore the Father's glory. These are the truths that radiate from the Collect for the Feast of the Transfiguration:

Almighty Father,
whose Son was revealed in majesty
   before he suffered death upon the cross:
give us faith to perceive his glory,
that we may be strengthened to suffer with him
and be changed into his likeness, from glory to glory;
who is alive and reigns with you and the Holy Spirit,
one God, now and for ever.[1]

In praying through the revelation of Moses and Elijah upon Sinai and Carmel I was reminded of the giant peaks of Kedarnath and Badrinath in Rudyard Kipling's beautiful Indian novel *Kim*. The boy Kim, in his long and faithful journey with the questing Lama, would gaze upon him, and the Lama

   … would stretch out his hands yearningly towards the high snows of the horizon. In the dawn they flared windy-red above dark blue, as Kedarnath and Badrinath, kings of that wilderness, took the first sunlight. All day long they lay like molten silver under the sun ... For all their marching Kedarnath and Badrinath were not impressed: and it was only after days of travel that Kim, uplifted upon some insignificant 10,000 foot hummock, could see that a shoulder knot or horn of the two great lords had – ever so slightly – changed outline.

These giant mountain peaks were majestic in wonder and glory, impressive in their grandeur, yet they were only the symbol of the Lama's higher quest, which was ineffable and beyond imagination. So is the glory of our Lord Jesus, in whom the mighty Yahweh himself became incarnate, so that symbols of height and depth, transcendence and profundity are lost in the dazzling light that defies all definition.

We have to begin simply and humbly in the stories and parables of the Gospels, in the compassionate words and healing works of the man Jesus. If we have watched, listened, believed and trusted thus far, we shall come to believe that perhaps this man is the Messiah, the longed-for deliverer who is to liberate the people and initiate the reign of peace.

But there arrives a moment, in all three synoptic Gospels, when Jesus takes his disciples aside and begins to share with them the approaching shadow of the Cross. Peter has just confessed Jesus as Messiah, the Christ of God, and they are all suddenly filled with the old prophecies of glory, even of power and conquest. Then they are jolted into reality:

He sternly ordered and commanded them not to tell anyone, saying, 'The Son of Man must undergo great suffering, and be rejected by the elders, chief priests and scribes, and be killed and on the third day be raised' (Luke 9:21f.).

It was not so much *what* he said – in any case they could not take that in at the moment – but it was the *manner* in which he said it, and the consequent enshrouding shadow that seemed to encircle and descend upon them.

Now as we walk in the footsteps of these disciples about a week later, we find ourselves leaving nine of them, and accompanying Peter, James and John, as Jesus leads them from the plain, gently ascending Mount Tabor.[2]

The disciples knew that there was something strange, something different, something momentous about this ascent, this mountain and this meeting with the inevitable reality that lay in the cloud of unknowing for them. The height of Tabor did not threaten them with physical exposure and altitude sickness, nevertheless it is a good metaphor for the fear and shivering awe that increasingly possessed mind and body.

Before taking up his present role as Principal of Edwardes College at Peshawar in Pakistan, a friend, Robin, led a Sixth Form expedition to Mount Kenya. He talked with me at my hermitage in his retreat preparation, sharing his hopes and fears. A few weeks later a letter arrived, describing the Kami Camp at 15,000 feet, dominated by a harsh world of glaciers, moraine and rock. Excitement and anticipation mingled with apprehension as doubts flooded in and dangers loomed all around. But there was no return and the restless night ended with the 5.30 a.m. rise. His letter translates his words into my own fears and apprehensions on the spiritual mountain journey:

You feel rotten at that hour, particularly at 15,000 feet. At that moment part of me would have willingly given up – wanted to escape from the trap of circumstance. But another part of me wanted to get on. We set off round the base of the peak to the foot of the North Face. Felt awful, puffing and panting, body protesting at such exertion at this early hour. Then came the first pitches, apprehension gives way to delight as the sun shines and the climbing goes well. We gain height. Sudden difficult bits dent one's optimism. The cloud comes in, cold sets in, tiredness returns, more doubts emerge but we continue. The climb has a momentum all its own. The mountain nudges, and goads and lures us upwards. The hard moves at about half height are climbed, we go higher. Now we feel committed – no turning back now. The nagging verticality below eats into the consciousness. I think mountain men learn to shut out height and exposure. People often say, 'I couldn't do that, I'm scared of heights.' I think we are all scared of heights, only the climber learns to blot it out.

Anyway, on we go and finally in the later afternoon we arrive at our bivvy site. A perch held up in the clouds, teetering on the edge of the summit ridge. Isolation. The swooping North Face, the complex of arêtes and towers leading to one single summit. One high place. One. I am occupied with simplicities. Chipping ice from cracks, melting it for water, eating, sleeping. There is exhilaration with the beauty and grandeur of the place. The cloudscape below us is breathtaking, so are the stars after dark, so many of them, so clear, so cold, so remote. All these impressions make up a fantastic world – very much 'other' than our normal world – the world of the valleys and plains and business as usual, homely and comfortable. This is different.

Robin is still a climber, but his primary task in Pakistan is a somewhat different mountain at present. What he shared geographically in that letter we still share spiritually, for we are both on the climb!

Peter, James and John would have said of the Tabor climb: 'This is different!' We are Easter people, we live on the glory side of the Passion and Resurrection, so we shall be able to interpret as we go along. But we must also endeavour to feel the strange loneliness, fear and awe of the chosen three as they are enveloped in Tabor's mystery.

Luke seems to indicate that it was evening, for the disciples were heavy with sleep, but as Jesus was held in silent prayer they tried to accompany him in spirit. They were not sure how or when it happened, but as he was praying, the appearance of Jesus was transformed and his garments became dazzling white. Both Matthew and Mark use the word *metamorpheo* from which our word *transfiguration* comes. The same verb root is used for the renewed mind and heart of the believing Christian (Romans 12:2), and for the radiant power of the Spirit who transforms us from one degree of glory to another (2 Corinthians 3:18).

The disciples gazed upon the glorious, radiant, transfigured Jesus and were filled with wonder. How much it reminds me of my first love for Christ as a boy, when his glory flooded my being and I used to sing with radiant joy in my heart:

> Turn your eyes upon Jesus
> Look full in his wonderful face,
> And the things of earth will grow strangely dim
> In the light of his glory and grace

Seeking the Will of God

Many things were happening on the mountain of transfiguration, but as the Collect reminded us, the shadow of the Cross had fallen across Jesus' path. After his baptism, driven into the wilderness, he had rejected all worldly and ambitious ploys to gain power or win favour. It had become clear to him that his path was that of the suffering servant, and he knew that if he were to fulfil the role of Messiah for Israel, then the very word had to be emptied of its military and nationalistic accretions. He had already understood that such a Messiah would tread the path of suffering, and in some mysterious way that suffering would be redemptive. This was the basic impulse that drew him towards Tabor.

Luke says he went to pray (9:28f.), and within that

communion of prayer there was the question of confirmation for the way to Jerusalem and the Cross. The baptism, the temptation, the transfiguration – these were watershed moments in the experience of Jesus on his way to Calvary. Here on the holy mount the question was answered, the way confirmed, as he sought to bring his will into complete harmony with the will of the Father.

As the disciples rubbed their eyes and looked again, they saw that two great figures from the past had appeared – and it was clear (how did they know?) that these were Moses of Mount Sinai and Elijah of Mount Carmel. Moses had experienced something of the lesser radiance of glory when the skin of his face shone as he carried the tables of the law down from Sinai (Exodus 34:29), and Elijah, after the fire of Carmel, had communed with God not in earthquake, wind or fire, but in the still, interior voice that came to him in the cave (1 Kings 19:8–12).

There was something mysterious about the deaths of both these patriarchs. God buried Moses in an unknown grave below Mount Nebo (Deuteronomy 34:5f.), and Elijah was translated before Elisha's astonished gaze in a chariot and horses of fire (2 Kings 2:11). And it was believed that Elijah would be the forerunner of the Messiah when he came, and Moses would accompany him. And here they were!

If we ask why these two great figures were communing with Christ, we find that Luke gives us the answer: 'They appeared in glory and were speaking of his departure, which he was about to accomplish at Jerusalem' (9:31).

The Greek word for 'departure' is *exodos*, with reverberations of the Exodus of the people of Israel from Egypt, through the wilderness and into the Promised Land. And that is exactly what Jesus was proposing to do – and here was the confirmation. The greatest figures of Israel's past had come, summing up the covenant and the prophetic line, encouraging him and recognizing in him their own consummation and glory.

In our lesser mountains of decision we also are surrounded by the saints of God, both in the communion of saints and the angelic aids and witnesses. As Jesus was alone, yet not alone, so may we gain encouragement and help in our own questioning and need.

At this point, when the disciples should have remained silent in adoration and contemplative wonder, poor Peter was so scared that as the figures of Moses and Elijah were withdrawing into the dimension from which they had come, he burst out in his impetuous way: 'Master, it is good for us to be here, let us make three dwellings, one for you, one for Moses, and one for Elijah ...' (9:33).

He was trying to say and do the right thing as a man of action, when what was required right then was stillness, reverence and passivity. But the shadow side of Peter may have been wanting to avoid the path of suffering which had become clear previously at Caesarea Philippi (Mark 8:31–33), and to stay on the slopes of the holy mountain.

We need to get these things in perspective. There is a time for entering into the contemplative glory of Mount Tabor, for without communion with God there is no strength or vision for the lowly path of service and suffering. But there is a time when we must descend the mountain and take the path to Jerusalem and Calvary with firm resolution and courage. And that is what Jesus did.

The only response to Peter's intervention was that a luminous cloud overshadowed them, and 'they were afraid as they entered the cloud' (Luke 9:34). The confirmation of God himself follows on the encouragement of the patriarchs. In Israel's history the luminous cloud stood for the *Shechinah*, the radiant glory of God's presence. It led the people in the dark and menacing wilderness by day and night (Exodus 13:21f.); it covered the Tabernacle tent of meeting with visible glory (40:34f.); it descended on Sinai enveloping Moses (34:5), and it overwhelmed the priests and people at the dedication of Solomon's temple (1 Kings 8:10f.).

From the midst of that luminous cloud came the very voice of God: 'This is my Son, the Beloved; with him I am well pleased. Listen to him!' Here was the complete confirmation. Jesus was fully answered, and from that moment he set his face towards Jerusalem.

Descending the Mountain

Then there was silence. The glory, the radiance, the Old Testament figures, the cloud of glory – they all departed, and there was Jesus, as he had always been to the disciples. Matthew says: 'Jesus came and touched them, saying, "Get up and do not be afraid"' (17:7), and all three evangelists say that 'Jesus only' stood before them.

If we have Jesus only with us, we can ascend the dangerous mountain, we can walk the dark lowlands and we can even tread the valley of the shadow of death. The luminous light of Mount Tabor will shine in our darkness and lead us to the heart of Christ. It is significant how often, in both near-death experiences and conversion stories, Christ appears as a being of light. One of the loveliest of these is that of a man from the mountains of India, who disappeared mysteriously into the mountainous Tibet border in 1929.

He was Sadhu Sundar Singh, who was born into a Sikh family with an outstanding saintly mother who taught him the Bhakti tradition of Hinduism. As a boy, he learned by heart large portions of the Sikh *Granth Sahib* and the Hindu *Gita*. Sundar's mother died when he was in his early teens, and he was thrown into such grief and anger that he burned the Bibles of the local Christian missionaries.

His despair made him suicidal, and he stayed in his room for three days and nights. On the third night he prayed: 'Oh God, if there be a God, reveal yourself to me tonight.' He decided that if there was no answer he would lie down on the railway line so that the 5.00 a.m. train from Ludhiana would end his life.

He spent seven hours in meditation, and at 4.45 a.m. a bright cloud of light suddenly filled his room, and out of the brightness emerged the face and figure of Jesus. Sundar would not have been so surprised if it had been Krishna or one of his family gods, but he knew it was Jesus. And Jesus spoke to him in words reminiscent of the Saul of Tarsus story, but in Hindustani: 'How long are you going to persecute me? I died for you. For you I gave my life. You were praying to know the right way; why don't you take it? I am the Way.'

His attitude and life were transformed. It was a radical, evangelical conversion, and from that moment he adopted the saffron robe of the sadhu, the wandering holy man of India, but as a Christian. Like his Master, he wandered through the villages and mountains of India, possessing nothing, proclaiming Christ. He received comfort from those who would share food and shelter with him, and he attempted to penetrate Tibet over the dangerous mountains. When he was about 40 years of age he tried once more, and was seen on a high mountain trail leading into Tibet. But he has never been heard from or seen since – he is 'lost' in the mountains.[3]

The Holy Mountain in Retrospect

There are two responses to the whole Tabor experience manifested by the disciples. The first is silence. The feeling expressed at the end of the episode is a sacred silence – commanded by Jesus (Matthew 17:9; Mark 9:9), and kept by the disciples (Luke 9:36) until Jesus had risen from the dead.

In the Church of God it is often distressing to see and hear the loud claims of tele-evangelists and healing crusades from the fundamentalist wing, and the weeping Madonnas or bleeding crucifixes from the Catholic wing. There are responsible and irresponsible people at both extremes, and they are also to be found among the pseudo-mystics with their stories of visions, swooning, trances and levitation. The mystical tradition is quite clear. Charisms of ecstasy, prophecy, miracles and healing are not the important things, and they ought not to be heralded. The communion of love between the believer and the Lord is the primary thing, and over-flowing compassion towards human beings and the created order follows from it. All other mystical charisms and gifts must be subservient to that primary experience and are not important in themselves.

To have accompanied Christ on the holy mountain was a sacred experience, and not one to be boasted about or even discussed. It is not to be spoken about until after the Resurrection when it becomes part of the gospel pattern and can be taken up by the writing evangelists and take its place in the whole tradition.

It is part of our privilege and task to openly proclaim the great facts of the gospel, and to add our own witness to its saving power, but we must be careful in gossiping abroad those sacred moments in which God has revealed himself to us in precious experiences of suffering or glory.

Jacopone da Todi, that most exhibitionist and enthusiastic of thirteenth-century Franciscan friars, also had a secret life of devotion. One of his poems 'Love that is Silent' [4] speaks of the secret joy of the indwelling love of Christ in the most profound and intimate communion with God. He goes on to say that if this love is not scattered abroad but secretly treasured it will glow more ardently. But if the believer shouts it and babbles it in the secular marketplace, it will be betrayed and lost to the one who previously held it close. Silence is the counsel, and a tender cultivation of the mystical love of Christ.

Jacopone does not mean that the gospel should not be proclaimed, experienced, communicated and shouted from the housetops. After all, it is an open secret, and it is God's will that all should be saved. He is speaking rather of the charisms of the Spirit and the communion of love which is between the believer and the Lord, between the Church and her heavenly Bridegroom. The inner secret of the transfigured Jesus belonged in that category of intimate communion within the fellowship of the three disciples 'so they kept the matter to themselves' (Mark 9:10). We shall note a similar attitude among the early Franciscans about the stigmata wounds which St Francis bore in his body.

Before we leave the mountain, there is a significant reference to the Transfiguration in the most neglected book of the New Testament. It is found in 2 Peter 1:16–18, where Peter is speaking of the Second Coming of Christ in glory, in the face of critics and doubters.

This epistle was not accepted into the canon until late in the third century, and is thought not to be by the apostle. It does seem to have come from a Petrine school or circle much later, but this particular section claims to have come from Peter's hand and inserted by the redactor into the completed epistle.

The point which is being made is the second response to the story of the Transfiguration – and that is its celebration. The first response was silence until the Resurrection, but then it is to be remembered, recorded and celebrated within the fellowship of believers. Peter is saying that not only is the transfigured body of Christ a foretaste of his immortal and resurrection body, but it is the foretaste of the *Parousia*, the coming of Christ to transfigure his people in the fullness of participation in the life of God (2 Peter 1:24).

The Eastern Orthodox churches hold this feast in special regard, calling it *Taborion* in commemoration of Mount Tabor. Happily, the Western Church celebrates it on the same day, 6 August. The most beautiful icons of the Transfiguration show the luminous central Christ on the mountain peak, with Moses and Elijah on either side caught up in the reflection of his glory, and the three disciples on the rocky slopes below.

The Transfiguration icon which faces me at my evening prayers today in my hermitage is one from the Palech school. The dazzling light of Christ has caused the three disciples to fall down on the slope of Tabor as if struck by lightning, and the accompanying text reads:

Your disciples contemplated your glory, O Lord God, so that seeing you crucified they would understand that you freely undertook your passion.

When the disciples were plunged into the sorrows of Christ's passion, this may well have been the experience which secretly and inwardly bore witness that the crucifixion was not the last word. And it is towards Mount Calvary that we now move.

Prayer

O God, who on the holy mount revealed to chosen witnesses your well-beloved Son, wonderfully transfigured, in raiment white and glistening:

Mercifully grant that we, being delivered from the disquietude of this world, may by faith behold the King in his beauty; who with you, O Father, and you, O Holy Spirit, lives and reigns, one God, for ever and ever. Amen.[5]

✳

Action:

Ask yourself two questions: (1) Do I spend any time in contemplative prayer, meditation and silence in my Christian life? (2) If so, does such communion in prayer energize the practical works of compassion in which I engage as a Christian?

If there is an honest negative answer to either of these questions, it is time you took the discipline of prayer (personal and communal) more seriously.

Talk with your church peer group, with priest/pastor, and join (or start) a meditation group, with a morning and evening time of meditation in your personal and family life.[6]

8

Mount Calvary

The Victory of Love: Luke 23:26–49

As they led him away, they seized a man, Simon of Cyrene, who was coming from the country, and they laid the cross on him, and made him carry it behind Jesus ... Two others also, who were criminals, were led away to be put to death with him. When they came to the place that is called the Skull, they crucified Jesus there with the criminals, one on his right and one on his left. Then Jesus said, 'Father, forgive them; for they do not know what they are doing.'

Stature of a Mountain

None of the biblical mountains we have been traversing have reached anything like the great nine Nepalese peaks or the great five Karakoram peaks, all of which tower over 8,000 metres (over 26,000 feet). And yet these biblical mountains are giants because they have been the places of revelation, where the divine transcendence has descended to human finitude, and where the mystic presence of God has met human need.

Mount Calvary is not even a high hill, but has been called Mount Calvary from the fourth century onwards because it was set upon a skull-like mound named Golgotha (lit. cranium). And yet it was here, not on one of those giant

8,000-metre peaks that the most terrible and most beautiful of all happenings took place. We are called upon to climb this mountain, and to gaze upon this wonder:

> Calvary's mournful mountain view,
>   There the Lord of Glory see,
> Made a sacrifice for you,
>   Dying on the accursed tree:
> 'It is finished!' hear him cry;
> Trust in Christ and learn to die.[1]

It is a humbling experience to read of the great mountaineers who have caught the vision of the towering peak of their childhood days, and have been haunted by it all their days. Some of them perished in the great adventure of climbing, and some of us have tried to follow in their steps on lowlier hills. But the vision that captured Christ's heart was Mount Calvary, and when 'he set his face to go to Jerusalem' (Luke 9:51), it was because he was destined to accomplish the world's redemption there.

George Mallory, that mysterious and tragic pioneer who died on Everest in June 1924, was asked a year earlier by a *New York Times* journalist: 'Why did you want to climb Mount Everest?' His answer, which has perplexed and stimulated the world ever since, was: 'Because it's there!' If we were to ask the Christ why he opened wide his arms on the Cross at Calvary, he would direct us to the mystery in the heart of God:

> For God so loved the world that he gave his only Son, so that everyone who believes in him may not perish but may have eternal life (John 3:16).

The journalist was so impressed by Mallory's answer that he went on to write of him:

This quiet young man's casual comment raises the ghost of such a tremendous adventure as the fireside mind can scarce conceive; of crawling along knife edges in the teeth of a bitter wind; of chopping footholds up the face of a wall of ice; of moving on where each step may reasonably be expected to be the last, and yet taking that step, and the next, and the next, and the next after that; of pushing up and up in spite of labouring heart and bursting lungs, until death is certain just ahead, and then turning back just as steadily, to wait for the next opportunity.[2]

As we follow in the steps of Jesus, we shall become aware of the love that burned in his heart and drove him on, in spite of the physical suffering, the mental anguish and the spiritual desolation, for 'was it not necessary that the Christ should suffer these things and then enter into his glory?' (Luke 24:26).

The Calvary Road

We pick up the journey as the soldiers lead Jesus out of the praetorium where they had mocked him with purple robe, crown of thorns and reed sceptre, all strange symbols of regal power and bearing, though not understanding what they were doing.

Jesus had been cruelly flogged with a long lash studded with sharpened pieces of bone and lead pellets. Such scourging reduced the body to strips of raw flesh and bleeding weals, and some men went mad or even died under it. He had then been delivered to the mockery of the soldiers through the whole night, and he was thrust forth, bearing the cross-beam on which he would be crucified.

Therefore, at the beginning of the *Via Dolorosa*, the Way of Sorrows, he staggered and fell, exhausted beneath the weight; one of the soldiers conscripted Simon, from Cyrene in distant North Africa, to bear the cross-beam for Jesus.

Simon may have fulfilled the ambition of a lifetime in coming from his homeland for the Jerusalem Passover – and now he was compelled to this awful task.

But the story for him does not end there. Rather, it is a new beginning. Mark tells us that he was the father of Alexander and Rufus (15:21), so they must have been known as believers when Mark wrote his Gospel. Moreover, Paul writes to the Roman church: 'Greet Rufus, chosen in the Lord; and greet his mother – a mother to me also' (16:13). Then again in Acts 13:1 there is a list of godly men among whom is named Simeon (Simon) called Niger – the usual name at that time for a man of dark skin from Africa.

The conclusion is that at some point Simon became a believer – and it surely began when he accompanied Jesus on the Calvary road, and bore his Cross. Can you imagine the story as he told it back home to his wife and children, and down through the years related that precious journey as he followed his Lord, bearing his cross?

So they came to the place of a skull. The four evangelists simply say 'they crucified him'. Crucifixion has been called the most cruel and horrible torture ever inflicted upon a human being. It originated in Persia, but it was from Carthage that the Romans learned it, though they only used it for treason and the lowest criminals – never for a Roman citizen.

The Cross was laid on the ground, and the prisoner was nailed upon it. Between the legs was a ledge of wood called the saddle to take his weight, otherwise the nails would have torn through the flesh of his hands. And there the prisoner hung to die slowly of hunger and thirst, sometimes becoming mad in the process.

It was at the third hour that Jesus was crucified, which was nine o'clock in the morning, and though he was offered some drugged wine by a group of Jerusalem women, he refused it.

The first words we hear Jesus say are: 'Father, forgive them; for they do not know what they are doing' (Luke 23:34).

Forgive whom? The soldiers who carried out their duty? Yes, certainly them. The Roman authorities of state who pronounced such a cruel execution through the cowardly Pilate? Yes, those too, caught up in the world-system of military might and political oppression. The Jewish church authorities in their religious inquisition, who had cold-bloodedly purposed this all along? Yes, those too, for had not Jesus said: 'Love your enemies and pray for those who persecute you ...' (Matthew 5:44)? The vacillating, violent, curious, perplexed, innocent and mixed crowd? Yes, certainly them, for they were like sheep without a shepherd.

Forgiveness is at the heart of the Cross. The One who openly, lovingly and willingly forgives all those who have abused and crucified him also opens his arms to a whole world of lost and wounded sinners, crying: 'Come to me all you that are weary and are carrying heavy burdens, and I will give you rest' (Matthew 11:28).

It sounds strange, in this context, to speak of Jesus giving rest when he was suffering exhaustion leading to mortal pain, and to speak of his universal love and forgiveness when he was transfixed by nails to a gibbet. It was sin that nailed Jesus to the Cross – but it was love that kept him there.

Again, his enemies had unconsciously acknowledged the truth, for above his head was the Roman *titulus* placed there by Pilate: 'This is Jesus, the King of the Jews' (Matthew 27:37). It was written in Latin, the language of government and power, in Greek, the language of unity, culture and commerce, and in Hebrew, the language of religion – universal in its scope.

If Jesus is acknowledged king, all these dimensions can be cleansed, forgiven and renewed. But if he is rejected, then government turns to violence and coercion, culture becomes corrupt and immoral, and religion begets bigotry, persecution and killing in the name of God. Luke suddenly catches a glimpse of one moment when he tells us that the people beheld him, the rulers derided him, and the soldiers mocked him (23:35f.). The watching that the soldiers carried out was partly their duty, and yet it was Jesus who was watching them in the sense that his outstretched arms were protecting that whole crowd, and the whole world from the results of their own failures and wickedness. Studdart Kennedy catches the mood in his poem 'He was a gambler too':

> And sitting down they watched him there,
> The soldiers did;
> There while they played with dice,
> He made his Sacrifice,
> And died upon the Cross to rid
> God's world of sin.
> He was a gambler too, my Christ,
> He took his life and threw
> It for a world redeemed.
> And ere his agony was done,
> Before the westering sun went down,
> Crowning that day with its crimson crown,
> He knew that he had won.[3]

Jesus in the Midst

One of the taunts mentioned by all three synoptic writers was: 'He saved others; he cannot save himself'. By including these words the evangelists show again the truth hidden beneath the mockery. The very point was that in saving others he had to give himself up to death, for the only way to wear the crown of glory was to bear the crown of thorns.

There is no coercion here. It is love freely offered and can only freely be received. Jesus was crucified between two criminals, and it is here that Luke tells us the story of salvation and rejection right at the foot of the Cross where he intends that we stand in our own decision. Old Bishop Ryle said that one thief was saved that none need despair – but only one, that none need presume. Jesus is in the midst, and should be the centre of love and adoration, but here he is the divider between those who embrace love and those who reject it. The old paschal hymn 'Beneath the Cross of Jesus' [4] puts it like this:

> There lies beneath its shadow,
>   But on the further side,
> The darkness of an open grave
>   That gapes both deep and wide;
> And there between us stands the Cross
>   Two arms outstretched to save,
> Like a watchman set to guard the way
>   From that eternal grave.

And here is the mystery of human choice and responsibility. Jesus hangs there both to *open* the gate of Paradise and to *guard* the way from eternal darkness. Jesus did not reject the thief who reviled him, but included him in the covering love of Calvary, forgave him freely for his insurrection, derision and rejection. But what Jesus would not, could not, do was to compel him to enter Paradise.

If there is one post-Easter scripture we should write over the whole Calvary scene it would be this one: 'In Christ God was reconciling the world to himself' (2 Corinthians 5:19). Everyone is included, no one is turned away by Jesus, even though they reject him. Yet, though he does not turn them away but rather invites them in spite of everything, if they *will not* enter in, then they will not!

What is there for the man or woman who *ultimately* rejects love, life and light, but to lapse into the non-being of unloving, darkness and annihilation? The rejection of the gospel of life and immortality is the falling into separation and death.

Both these crucified men are transfixed in a place where there is no movement, with the same opportunity for grace, the same offer of salvation simply on the grounds of mercy and unbounded love. The 'good thief' surely did not understand how the crucified Jesus could be king, but he recognized that Jesus was regal, lifted upon the throne of the Cross and crowned with dying glory, and he made a leap of faith – where else was there to go? He cried, 'Jesus, remember me when you come into your kingdom,' and Jesus replied, 'Truly I tell you, today you will be with me in Paradise' (23:42f.). How impossible, but how marvellously true.

These two seem to be insurrectionists, revolutionaries, and the second one deliberately held on to his mindset even as death was looking him in the eyes. It was possible to get into such a state of mind and heart that his nationalistic liberation ideology, backed up by violent, political revolution, was the only way of salvation he could envisage. That is what 'messiah' meant to him, and if Jesus was impotent to liberate them from their present suffering and predicament and take the kingdom by storm, then he could only despise such impotence and even in his dying moments cling stubbornly to a philosophy which he seemed unable to relinquish.

Is there hope for such as him? Well, I do believe that the only thing that keeps a soul out of heaven is the rejection of love. If ideologies, philosophies and mindsets hold us in their grip, and if the hypocritical church does not communicate Jesus' reconciling love and mercy in this life, then perhaps beyond the vale of death there is another opportunity, another communication of God in which the two ways are made perfectly clear. The invitation of gracious love may then be set forth so plainly that the sheer contrast between life and death, light and darkness, truth and error, cannot be confused. If *then* love is deliberately rejected, then lostness is freely chosen and it may be said: 'This is the judgement, that the light has come into the world, and people loved darkness rather than light because their deeds were evil' (John 3:19).

Mary at the Cross

The monastery at Glasshampton, where my hermitage is situated, is dedicated to 'St Mary at the Cross', and just before we consider the darkness that descended on the hill of Calvary for those last three hours, let us turn to those three beautiful verses found only in John's Gospel (19:25–27):

> When Jesus saw his mother and the disciple whom he loved standing beside her, he said to his mother, 'Woman, here is your son.' Then he said to the disciple, 'Here is your mother.' And from that hour the disciple took her into his own home.

In my hut chapel I have a large reproduction of the Crucifix that spoke to St Francis at the church of St Damiano and that was the stimulus to his conversion. On the right of the Saviour stand Mary and John beneath his wounded side, the water symbolizing our baptism, and the blood symbolizing his cleansing power and the eucharist.

The mighty task which Christ was accomplishing in his passion and death was the work of our salvation, and we have already been aware of the powerful things which were taking place on Mount Calvary. But right in the midst of it, when her dear Son was hanging in pain and desolation, there drew near Mary his mother, with John the disciple and that faithful group of women. The 13th-century hymn, thought to be from the hand of Jacopone da Todi, begins:

> At the Cross her station keeping,
> Stood the mournful Mother weeping,
>   Close to Jesus at the last.
> Through her soul, of joy bereavèd,
> Bowed with anguish, deeply grievèd,
>   Now at length the sword has passed.

As they stood in silent sorrow at the Cross, Mary and John were held within the circle of Calvary love. Jesus gave them both into one another's keeping, and this is John the evangelist's way of drawing us into this circle of loving communion as we share the sorrow of our Saviour's death.

Then we may identify ourselves with John the disciple loving Jesus to the end, and feel our intimate affinity with Mary as the mother-figure of the Church. Not only do we give reverence and honour to Mary as the mother of our Lord, but in her we see that we are not separate believers, but a part of the communion of saints and of the eucharistic fellowship, members of the Body of Christ.

At the foot of the Cross we enter into the pain and sorrow of Mary and John, and as our tears mingle with theirs, in the very fellowship of grief we find some relief and even a ray of hope.

Darkness over the Whole Land

The three evangelists bring us at last to the deep darkness that pervaded the land from midday to three in the afternoon. They intend us to understand that this was cosmic darkness, that nature itself was in mourning for the terrible thing that was happening on that first Good Friday.

Just as Jesus had predicted, he had been taken by the hands of wicked men and crucified, and the evangelists mean us to see that there were malign forces behind the acting authorities, and a cosmic drama was being enacted on the hill of Calvary.

There are two cries of Jesus which are important for us to hear in the darkness. The first is the heart-rending 'My God, my God, why have you forsaken me?' (Mark 15:34). This seems to be a most terrible cry in the mouth of the One who had always trusted his heavenly Father and felt continually the warmth and comfort of his presence, even in times of hostility and rejection. What can it mean?

First we find that it is the opening verse of Psalm 22, and this psalm is woven into the whole crucifixion narrative. Further on we read: 'All who see me mock at me; they make mouths at me, they wag their heads' (22:7); and then: 'they divide my clothes among themselves, and for my clothing they cast lots' (22:18).

In the dark places of his pain and suffering Jesus may have been repeating the psalm which had been in his heart since childhood, and now in such extremity he was repeating, mumbling, even crying this psalm in utter need, for even in his own depths he knew it led from desolation to hope.

But there is something far deeper here. It is the mystery of the Lamb of God bearing away the sins of the world. The Early Church believed that Jesus, as Messiah, was the Suffering Servant of Isaiah 53, who took upon himself the whole burden of human sin. There is a very beautiful passage in which Paul writes of the forgiving and reconciling work of Christ, ending with the daring and mysterious words: 'For our sake he made him to be sin who knew no sin, so that in him we might become the righteousness of God' (2 Corinthians 5:16–21).

Following this divine mystery of sin-bearing, there is something that is also profoundly human. It is that Christ descended into the darkest depths, exhausted the most desolate places of loneliness and pain, and plumbed the abyss of physical, mental and spiritual agony and dereliction. In other words, we can sink to no depths he has not traversed before, and we can enter no experience of loneliness or fear that he has not known and purged by his presence and love. Such knowledge not only assures us of the forgiveness of our sins and comforts us in our loneliness and distress, but it gives us strength and peace in the face of death – and beyond.

The second cry is called a great shout, and is referred to in all four Gospels. It is not simply a shout of a crucified man reaching his last moments, but a shout of triumph. John goes further and tells us that what he shouted was the cry of victory, '*Tetelestai*', which we translate with the three words: 'It is finished'. It is the cry of one who has completed his work, achieved his goal, won the battle and finished the race. Darkness has given way to eternal light, and morning has broken.

There is a final word, and it is one which I repeat or sing each night at Compline before going to sleep: 'Father, into your hands I commend my spirit.' If there is one image I want before me as I die it is that of the dying Jesus resigning his spirit into the hands of his heavenly Father. It enables me to realize that one day I shall be called upon to make such a resignation. I shall have to let go my physical life and the world which has brought me both joy and sorrow, and make that last pilgrimage at Mount Calvary, into the eternal Love from which I came and to which I go. I practise it each night in the quiet darkness for myself and my loved ones, and I commend it to you.

Mount Calvary and Mount Alverna

From Mount Calvary we conclude by moving through the centuries to the year 1224 when St Francis of Assisi climbed the Mount Alverna where he received the stigmata, the wounds of Jesus in his body and spirit.

Francis was 42 years old, and from the age of 23, when he heard the call of Christ from the St Damiano Crucifix, he had surrendered everything to the Saviour. He has been called 'the only perfect Christian'[5] and certainly he is universally acknowledged as one who followed most closely the footsteps of Jesus in life and death.

Francis had made a long and exhausting pilgrimage to Mount Alverna in Tuscany, for he believed that there he had a divine appointment with Christ. On the way, three times he asked his faithful disciple Leo to open the gospel book for guidance, and three times it opened at the passion of Christ.

This confirmed Francis' guidance, but he needed to know that his action was in concert with the will of God, and not simply some personal aberration.

When at last they arrived at this rugged and solitary mountain, Francis began his 40 days of prayer and fasting. On Holy Cross Day 1224, we find him kneeling before his rough hut, supported by a rock and facing east just before the rising of the sun. With tears he prayed this prayer:

> My Lord Jesus Christ, I pray You to grant me two graces before I die; the first is that during my life I may feel in my soul and in my body, as much as possible, that pain which You, dear Jesus, sustained in the hour of Your most bitter Passion. The second is that I may feel in my heart, as much as possible, that excessive love with which You, O Son of God, were inflamed in willingly enduring such suffering for us sinners.[6]

You see what he asked? First, that he may feel the *pain* of Jesus' passion, and secondly, that he may feel the *love* of Jesus' passion. Simple, direct and aweful. Our prayers are rarely so direct and certainly are not prepared for such radical risk in loving. Here is the account that Bonaventure gives of what happened next. Francis was held for some time within the tender yearning of prayer, and then:

> Suddenly, from the height of heaven, a Seraph having six wings of flame swept down towards him. It appeared in the image of a man hanging on a cross. Two wings at the head, two others served for flight, and the last two covered the body. It was Christ Himself, who, in order to manifest Himself to the blessed one, appeared in this guise. It ... fixed Francis with its gaze, then left him, having imprinted on his flesh the living Stigmata of the Crucifixion. From this moment, indeed, Francis was marked with the wounds of the Divine Redeemer. His feet, his hands seemed pierced

with nails of which the round black heads appeared in the palms of the hands, and on the feet, the points thrust through the flesh bent back. And there, too, on the right side, was a wound as though made by a lance, from which the blood frequently oozed, even through his shirt and tunic.[7]

Francis tried to hide the wounds, but then in veiled terms he asked his few companions on the mountain whether he should hide a certain extraordinary favour which God had given him.

Illuminato sensed Francis' radiant joy and perplexity, and said, 'Brother, remember that when God reveals his secrets to you, it is not for yourself alone; they are intended for others too.'

Francis was aware of a certain intimate secrecy between the believer and the Lord which cannot be gossiped about with loss of affective communion. But he also realized that there was such a thing as an 'open secret' which could be shared reverently with the few who would understand, and be led nearer to God by such sharing. Within the Franciscan communities in the early days the stigmata episode was not one that was talked about openly, but kept primarily on the holy mountain, and shared with great reverence and care among the friars and Clare sisters.

Identification with the Crucified Christ

There is a great deal more which could be shared about Francis' identification with the wounds and suffering of Christ, but it is sufficient to affirm that Francis is among the first who reproduce in spirit and body the suffering and healing Jesus. Only those who have entered into the sorrows of Mount Calvary are able to witness and experience the transfigured wounds of healing in the Resurrection.

Francis lived only two years after Mount Alverna, but those years were filled with the radiant love and compassion that flowed from the wounds of Jesus. When Leo secretly spied on Francis in the woods before the stigmata, he found him kneeling in the moonlight with face and arms uplifted to heaven, repeating with fervour: 'Who are you, my dearest God? And who am I, a vile worm and your useless servant?' Then, as Leo looked on in awe and fear, he saw a flame of fire descend and envelop Francis.

Blood and fire are the signs of Christ's passion, and if we are to enter into the suffering of Christ for our world we shall bear his wounds. But it will not stop there, for from the fountainhead of such compassion and mercy healing will spring forth for the poor world in which we live. So as the disciples descended from Mount Tabor in transfiguring light, and as Francis and Leo returned to Assisi from Mount Alverna, so we shall descend from Mount Calvary filled with pity and with energy for the healing of our world's ills.

Prayer

Lord Jesus Christ: the wounds of your passion are now the wounds of glory, and your servant Francis bore those wounds with tears and love;

Enable us to enter into the sorrows of your Cross, and to bear within our hearts the wounds of your compassion;

Then we shall become channels of your peace and light in a world of conflict and darkness. Amen.

*

Action

Remember the words of Jesus that anything you do for others you do also for him, and that the early Franciscans worked among the lepers and outcasts of society.

Seek out a person, a group, a community who are suffering, and do your part to alleviate their suffering in a practical way, and in so doing be the hands and feet of Christ in the world.

9

Mount Olivet

Received into Glory: Acts 1:1–12

As they were watching, Jesus was lifted up, and a cloud took him out of their sight. While he was going and they were gazing up toward heaven, suddenly two men in white robes stood by them. They said, 'Men of Galilee, why do you stand looking up toward heaven? This Jesus, who has been taken up from you into heaven, will come in the same way as you saw him go into heaven.'

Ascending and Descending

In all the mountains we have traversed there has been an ascent and a descent, and this has been a quite literal movement – though there have been many spiritual metaphors surrounding the narratives. Here the ascent is somewhat different, and the promised returning descent has to be interpreted.

Our understanding of the physical nature of the world is radically different from pre-Copernican days and we do not live on a flat earth with heaven above the bright blue sky.

Nevertheless, we must not dismiss the resurrection and ascension stories as crude literalism. The New Testament writers were more sophisticated than some liberal scholars assume, and when they affirmed that Christ is seated at the right hand of the Father they knew, as Luther said, that the right hand of the Father is everywhere! For them, God is spirit and has no physical body nor material throne. C. S. Lewis once said that if you had asked his mother if she believed that Christ ascended into heaven, she would have responded: 'Oh yes – in a manner of speaking'. And those words 'in a manner of speaking' are a clue to an understanding of what the Gospels and epistles say about the risen body of Jesus. It is a body, but it is not mortal; it is the body that was crucified but it is now a spiritual body, capable of appearing and with-drawing – through closed doors.

In this chapter we stand with the disciples on the Mount of Olives just outside Jerusalem, and here it is that one chapter of experience ends, and another is about to begin.

Our previous Mount Calvary story showed what evil was perpetrated by a wicked world on the body of Jesus. In the eyes of the pre-Easter crowd that was the end of the prophetic proclamation and charismatic deeds of the One who was now broken in death. Luke speaks of the effect of the dark hours leading to the death of Jesus in this way:

> And when all the crowds who had gathered there for this spectacle saw what had taken place, they returned home, beating their breasts. But all his acquaintances, including the women who had followed him from Galilee, stood at a distance, watching these things (23:49).

Already, it is clear that only catastrophe and desolation are manifested in the worldly crowd, but there is a sense of 'waiting and watching' in that small group of followers. There was no doubt that Jesus was dead – the soldier who pierced his side made sure of that (John 19:34) – and Jesus was reverently placed in the garden tomb by Joseph of Arimathea and Nicodemus (John 19:38–42).

John's record of the happenings in the garden is powerful and convincing. Peter and John run to the cave-tomb after being told by Mary Magdalene that the stone had been rolled away and the body gone. They found the tomb empty but the grave wrappings lying exactly in place, implying that the body had passed through them, as it was later to pass through closed doors (20:1–10).

Mary returned and was confronted with the risen Jesus who she first thought to be the gardener, and his words to her, 'Do not touch me', indicate that though this is the same Jesus, his body has been transformed in its rising and is no longer bound by the space-time continuum which limits us all. She is to know him, from now on, as the risen Lord of life and death, present to his disciples everywhere:

> Do not hold on to me, because I have not yet ascended to the Father. But go to my brothers and say to them, 'I am ascending to my Father and your Father, to my God and your God' (20:17).

The next appearance is to the gathered disciples in the upper room where he turns their fears into joy, shows them his wounded yet risen body, and breathes the Holy Spirit of peace upon them. The report of such a stupendous happening is too much for Thomas who affirms his need for physical proof. A week later he is overwhelmed by Jesus entering through closed doors and offering his pierced hands and wounded side. 'My Lord and my God,' cries Thomas, as the evangelist records the objective reality of Jesus' risen body. It is the body that was crucified, yet palpably alive and immortal (20:19–29).

There are variations and even discrepancies in the Gospel narratives, but the basic affirmation of the risen body, the empty tomb and the vital power of the living, transfigured Lord is constant. It is a truth to be believed, but primarily it is an experienced relationship out of which emerges a joyful confession and a renewed life of love and witness.

Luke tells us the beautiful story of the two Emmaus

walkers whose eyes were not capable of recognizing him (24:16). Was it their grief, their unbelief or that the risen body was somehow different? Their eventual exciting amazement sent them post-haste to the upper room in Jerusalem, where we have the account of Jesus' appearance (24:36–49). There is no doubt here about the physical reality of Jesus' risen body: 'Look at my hands and my feet,' he says, 'see that it is I myself. Touch me and see; for a ghost does not have flesh and bones as you see that I have.'

After opening their minds to understand the scriptures, and commissioning them as witnesses to the suffering and risen Messiah, he promises to clothe them with the Holy Spirit of power in Jerusalem. Then he led them out to the Mount of Olives, and Luke's Gospel ends joyfully:

> And lifting up his hands he blessed them. While he was blessing them, he withdrew from them and was carried up into heaven. And they worshipped him, and returned to Jerusalem with great joy; and they were continually in the temple blessing God.

Ascending the Mountain

Luke is aware that he needs to carry on the story and that he has to fill out that last picture of his Gospel in which the group of transformed disciples returned from the mountain of ascension to the temple, full of praise and worship. He retells the ascension story, correcting and filling in details which are important for the future. So let us now look at some of these details.

First of all he has to correct their thinking about the kingdom of God and the place of the Messiah within it. This had always been difficult, but previously their misunderstanding was because they had interpreted these words traditionally and in political terms. This was a mountain they had to climb, because Jesus was not a political messiah, establishing a national kingdom by overthrowing the Romans by the might of God, and renewing the Davidic dynasty in Jerusalem as the centre of the world. Rather, his understanding of his role as Messiah was one in which the kingdom of love would be established, by suffering. His was a kingdom, but a kingdom of love, where God's will would be reflected on earth as it is in heaven, and where the Holy Spirit would be the unifying power. The promised Holy Spirit would be poured out upon the disciples and followers, creating the community of Christ's Body, his witnesses in Jerusalem, fanning out to Samaria and into the gentile world. They also had to learn that the word 'witness' was the same as that for 'martyr' and that present joy would soon be challenged by persecution and suffering.

In Luke's first chapter of the Acts they were still thinking in pre-Easter terms, in the ways of the old Israel. 'Lord, are you at this time going to restore the kingdom to Israel?' was the question. Jesus faced them resolutely, not denying the best of their yearnings for the prophetic promises of a kingdom of righteousness and peace on the mountain of the Lord, where the tears would be wiped from every eye, and Jerusalem would be filled with glory (Isaiah 25:6–10; Micah 4:1–4).

The kingdom was imminent and 'immediately to appear' (Luke 19:11), though not in the way they had expected. The disciples knew that the centre of Jesus' message was the proclamation of the kingdom of God (Mark 1:14), but they understood it in nationalistic terms. The Jews were conscious of their election, but apart from a discerning remnant, they interpreted it as an election to domination and not to service. Palestine was only the size of Wales and it had been subject in its history to the Babylonians, the Persians, the Greeks and now the Romans. Yet the Jews, including the disciples, still looked forward to a destiny of world sovereignty and political privilege.

The only thing that could change their minds and their hearts was a mighty act of intervention far greater than any political miracle, and to this their attention was now directed.

Jesus turned their attention away from date-fixing and literalizing the prophetic hope of Israel, and focused their minds on the imminent coming of the Holy Spirit which he, as exalted and glorified Lord, would send to enlighten and energize them. His last words made it clear:

> You will receive power when the Holy Spirit has come upon you; and you will be my witnesses in Jerusalem, in all Judea and Samaria, and to the ends of the earth (1:8).

Ascent from the Mountain

As they listened, the importance of Jesus' words impressed themselves upon the disciples. As they watched, their eyes opened wider, for something mysterious, something momentous, had happened. It is stated baldly and simply: 'As they were watching, he was lifted up, and a cloud took him out of their sight' (1:9). He was taken *from* the earth, and taken *into* glory. The earth is quite solid, tangible and literal, but the glory is a dimension beyond literal or even metaphorical images. We must use concrete and abstract language in rare combinations to speak of the spiritual world or else be completely silent, but all language falls short of the reality. So what we must not do is to think that Jesus went up like a first-century astronaut until he reached some *place*, some terminus, called heaven. Let us consider what the Ascension means.

There had to be an end to Jesus' resurrection appearances so that he could return to the glory which he shared with the Father before the foundation of the world (John 17:5). The 40 days had come to an end, and it had to be made clear that Jesus was being taken away, and Luke communicates to us the way in which the disciples experienced the parting – the lifting up into the cloud of glory.

We are no strangers to this cloud upon the mountain, and neither were the disciples. They would associate it with all the cloud appearances which we have noted in the history of God's people, indicating the presence and glory of God. Peter, James and John had entered into such a cloud on Mount Tabor when they saw Moses and Elijah with the central figure of Jesus transfigured in glory. It may well have been that this was the subject of their sharing with the other disciples on the return from Mount Olivet, for they were only bound to silence until the resurrection of Jesus.

We cannot, in our present state of knowledge, imagine the conditions of the glorified and transfigured human body of Jesus united with the Father in heaven. If the Old Testament cloud hid the mystery of Yahweh from human sight, so now the same *Shekinah* glory cloud conceals the exalted Saviour.[1] What was clear to the disciples was that Jesus had given his last instructions, and they were to wait in Jerusalem for the descent of the Holy Spirit from the same glory into which Christ had ascended.

Coming in Glory

Luke follows the description of the Ascension with the promise of the Second Coming of Christ. As their wide-open eyes saw the cloud receive Jesus, they were suddenly addressed by two men in white robes denoting their angelic mission. And they now had a gospel to proclaim; they must now lower their eyes to their mission upon earth which was to announce that the kingdom long promised would come, and the Messiah would return to inaugurate it in glory. They must not calculate times and seasons, but there is to be a divine event to which all creation moves, and they must prepare for it.

The task in hand is the proclamation and living out of the saving gospel of Christ. Further light and empowerment will be given them in the coming of the Holy Spirit, and this dynamic will fill them with energy and compassion to be the body of Christ in a lost and sin-sick world, groaning for redemption.

Luke is keen to tell us in Acts of their return to Jerusalem to find Jesus' mother and other followers, but in the account of the Ascension in the Gospel he simply communicates the mingling of reverence, wonder and adoration (24:52f.).

On Ascension Day in our friaries we have the Easter candle burning at the Eucharist. Following the reading of the Ascension Gospel account, one of the brothers used to take a snuffer and extinguish the flame to symbolize the 'taking away' of the bodily presence of Christ on Mount Olivet. I like this symbolism, but the practice is less frequent now because this 'absence' can be misunderstood. Such misunderstanding is made explicit in the somewhat equivocal hymn verse we used to sing at ordinations:

> So age by age, and year by year,
>   His grace is handed on;
> And still the holy Church is here,
>   Although her Lord has gone.[2]

Very odd! We are not celebrating the absence of Jesus, for he is more truly present than ever he had been in the days of his mortal body, for by the Holy Spirit his promise is experienced: 'Where two or three are gathered in my name, I am there among them' (Matthew 18:20).

Nevertheless we are living in the 'time between' the first and second advent of our Lord Jesus. He is simply not here in any bodily or physical sense, and we have to learn to live with a certain absence in our human and Christian experience, though we may want to sing 'I wish that his hands had been placed on my head, and his arms had been thrown around me'.[3]

What was it, then, that gave the disciples such joy and energy when they descended Mount Olivet and returned to Jerusalem? We look back on those early days of the New Testament church and we are able to affirm the basis of our joy and hope. First, we are part of the living Body of Christ, which is his Church on earth and in heaven. Second, that Church is sustained by his word in scripture and his presence in the Eucharist. Third, the same Holy Spirit who descended on the disciples at Pentecost indwells the Church and every believer today – enlightening and empowering. Fourth, with all these blessings we are called upon to proclaim the reconciling gospel in the world, and to live out lives of service and holiness, looking for and expecting the second advent of our Lord in glory. We must not indulge in speculating about dates or prophesying, but should live in the light of that coming and of the appearance of that kingdom in which Christ is called the Prince of Peace (Isaiah 9:8). That kingdom can be called Mount Zion, and to that mountain we shall now turn.

Prayer

Risen Lord of life and death: Help me to feel and know your presence with me in my daily life, and in the fellowship of your Church;

Grant me that sense of anticipation of your Second Advent which filled the early disciples, and let your Holy Spirit draw others to your love manifested in my life. Amen.

*

Action

Has the material in this chapter stimulated or perplexed your understanding of Jesus' ascension to the Father? Either way, it is a sign that you should study your Faith more seriously. What about doing more theological reading or joining a reading/study circle?

If one does not function in your church why not seek permission and get a group together for study and prayer?

Mount Zion

The Kingdom of God:
Isaiah 2:1–5; 11:1–9

In days to come the mountain of the LORD's house shall be established as the highest of the mountains, and shall be raised above the hills; all the nations shall stream to it. Many peoples shall come and say, 'Come, let us go up to the mountain of the LORD, to the house of the God of Jacob; that he may teach us his ways and that we may walk in his paths.' For out of Zion shall go forth instruction, and the word of the LORD from Jerusalem. He shall judge between the nations and shall arbitrate for many peoples; they shall beat their swords into ploughshares, and their spears into pruninghooks; nation shall not lift up sword against nation, neither shall they learn war any more. O house of Jacob, come, let us walk in the light of the LORD.

Mount Zion: Spiritual Jerusalem

What a mountain, and what a vision! It is the most glorious and the most difficult mountain that we face. Mount Zion is the geographical city of Jerusalem, and it is the symbolic name which fulfils and consummates the highest dreams and profoundest prophecies of the Old Testament. Jerusalem is the holy city of the three great world religions – Judaism, Christianity and Islam – and it continues to be the centre of conflict and religious and political persecution. Whatever our attitude towards its place in prophecy, we must continue to pray for the peace of Jerusalem and for all who profess to love her (Psalm 122:6).

In Jewish thinking in Jesus' time, the term 'Messiah' was intimately linked with Jerusalem as Mount Zion. One of the great problems that Jesus had with his disciples was the use of this word. It had political, military and violent overtones that Jesus wanted to avoid. He certainly did not see himself as a nationalist messiah with a vocation to overthrow the military rule of the Roman oppressor and set up a political and theocratic kingdom at Jerusalem, making Zion the centre of the world. The ideals and visions of the passages from Isaiah listed above understand Zion's kingdom and rule in entirely different terms to the violent Maccabaean dream.

In the ministry of Jesus we meet what is called 'the messianic secret'[1] when, in certain circumstances, Jesus forbade the use of the term messiah, and endeavoured to purify it of its nationalist and military associations. His understanding of the person and role of messiah was spiritual: the suffering saviour would abjure force of arms, calling God's people to repentance and new life in the kingdom of God. The mark of this kingdom was the rule of love and mercy here and now, with its ultimate fulfilment in heaven.[2] This was to be brought about not by the violent uprising of a zealot party led by a political, military messiah after the pattern of Judas Maccabaeus, but by the Suffering Servant who would take upon himself the burden of Israel's transgressions, defeating the powers of darkness by the power of love.[3]

Through the death and resurrection of Jesus and the descent of the Spirit at Pentecost, the apostles learned what kind of messiah Jesus really was.[4] It is significant that the Isaiah corpus which speaks of the future glory of Zion is the one which affirms a transcendent kingdom of peace and the role of the Suffering Servant.

Our task is to interpret the longings of the great prophets in the light of the new covenant in Christ. In so doing we shall see that the highest and best of the prophetic vision is fulfilled in the spiritual kingdom of universal peace which, in our own time, spills over into the practical international politics of reconciliation and peaceful co-existence. Only such a vision can transform racial hatreds into reconciliation in contemporary Zion – Jerusalem itself.

Mount Zion, as the centre of the earth, a universal religion and a perpetual peace, was the messianic hope of Israel, centred on Jerusalem. It sounds throughout the prophetic tradition of Israel, in both literal and spiritual terms. In the New Testament, the concept of Zion becomes the kingdom of God, and its universal and ultimate fulfilment is in the eternal dimension of heaven.

Jesus makes clear the transformation of the meaning of Mount Zion in his meeting with the woman of Samaria in the fourth chapter of John. At one point she attempted to move the conversation away from her personal life to religion and wanted to talk about the merits of Mount Zion (Jerusalem) over against those of Mount Gerazim. As a Samaritan she was committed to Gerazim as the location of divine focus of worship.[5] But Jesus breaks in with his radical understanding of true worship, bound neither to religious institutions or geographical location:

> Woman, believe me, the hour is coming when you will worship the Father neither on this mountain nor in Jerusalem … the hour is coming, and is now here, when the true worshippers will worship the Father in spirit and truth, for the Father seeks such as these to worship him. God is Spirit, and those who worship him must worship in spirit and truth (John 4:21–24).

Later, we find St Paul writing to the gentile Galatian Christians that Jerusalem is the free mother of us all

(Galatians 4:26f.). Some decades after the Jerusalem temple was destroyed in AD70, the Apocalypse speaks of the 'New Jerusalem' which is the eternal holy city for the redeemed of all nations (Revelation 21:9–22:5).

There is a powerful key passage in the Epistle to the Hebrews (12:18–29), in which earthly Mount Sinai is contrasted with its fearful demands of law and fiery justice, with the heavenly Jerusalem – the new Zion of grace and joy in the consummated kingdom:

> But you have come to Mount Zion and to the city of the living God, the heavenly Jerusalem, and to innumerable angels in festal gathering, and to the assembly of the firstborn who are enrolled in heaven, and to God the judge of all, and to the spirits of the righteous made perfect, and to Jesus, the mediator of a new covenant, and to the sprinkled blood that speaks of a better word than the blood of Abel.

The Zion psalms are full of the hope and confidence of the pilgrims approaching the holy city:

> Those who trust in the LORD are like Mount Zion,
>   which cannot be moved, but abides forever.
> As the mountains surround Jerusalem,
>   so the LORD surrounds his people, from this
>   time on and for evermore (125:1f.).

Isaac Watts takes up the theme in his Gospel Zion hymn:

> How pleased and blest was I
>   To hear the people cry,
> 'Come, let us seek our God today!'
>   Yes, with a cheerful zeal
>   We haste to Zion's hill,
> And there our vows and homage pay.[6]

Political Zionism

We must be careful not to interpret certain Old Testament prophecies as part of a literal, nationalist and political programme for today, for this would land us in immense moral and political difficulties. Any religious claim which is exclusive, in which God 'is on our side', and we become 'the arm of the Lord', leads to religious wars and bloodshed. This has been the bane of Judaism, Islam and Christianity. It is the shame of religious people, and a blasphemous rejection of the God we profess to serve: the God and Father of our Lord Jesus Christ.

I sang Isaac Watts' Mount Zion hymn a few days ago in my hermitage. In singing of Zion as the city of reconciliation, peace and joy, I was saddened at how far this is from the reality of today's Jerusalem. Instead of being the holy city, it has become a place of divisions and ethnic violence and oppression.

The expulsion of the Jews from Jerusalem took place in AD 135, and the consequent yearning for Zion filled the minds and prayers of exiled Jews from that time. I cannot help praying for God's ancient people and loving them, for our Saviour came from the stock of David and Jewish people have been the suffering scapegoat among the nations through the centuries. Nevertheless, neither from the New Testament nor from a contemporary Christian standpoint am I persuaded that political Zionism is the fulfilment of Old Testament prophecies.

A friend, Roger, is deeply involved with Jewish-Christian relations and is just off to a Church Leaders' Conference in Israel. Among the conference themes are the religious response to the Holocaust, and the thorny question of the State of Israel. We have been doing some background reading, and I would commend two particular books relevant to this chapter. The first is Kenneth Cragg's book, *Palestine, the Prize and Price of Zion*, which is a serious and objective study by a sympathetic Christian. The second is David Goldberg's book, *To the Promised Land*, which is a history of Zionist thought by a Jewish author.[7] I have indicated to Roger my unease about the way in which some Christians seem to see the formation of Israel's secular state in 1948 as a direct fulfilment of biblical prophecies. This entails approving of anything modern secular Israel does: its treatment of the Palestinians, its nuclear capability and the activities of Mossad.

Christian biblical interpretation is littered with fundamentalist groups seeing in certain contemporary events a literal fulfilment of ancient prophecies. All kinds of political intrigue and military violence may be justified in pressing the fulfilment of such prophetic words. There is, of course, a danger in simply 'spiritualizing' the prophetic word into an ethereal dimension in which we may evade practical responsibility against political abuse and racial injustice. But I find myself agreeing with Roger on this:

I believe we should read the Old Testament – and everything else – 'through Jesus Christ our Lord', and that in the New Testament, the inheritance, the *kleronomia*, is no longer the land, but the kingdom of God. I agree with you about not spiritualising, but an interpretation of the Old Testament which sees its fulfilment in the return of the Jews seems to me to bypass Christ. Of course, from a Jewish perspective it is legitimate – but not accepted by all Jews. Yet that leaves Christians with no theology of territory which I think we need. As David Dimbleby said on a TV programme on South Africa, 'The trouble with all promised lands is that someone else has always got there first.' It follows that we need a positive theology of the 'other' who is so often ignored or demonised. We have done this to the Jews for two thousand years. When the oppressed become the oppressors they know exactly what to do.[8]

Mount Zion in Eschatology

As we work out how to climb this particular mountain, a
great part of the answer is summed up in the word 'escha-
tology'. This word means 'last things', and relates to the
kingdom of God in its eternal dimension. Of course, the
kingdom is already present wherever the will of God is done.
Indeed the kingdom came with the life and work of Christ,
and in the establishment of the Church as the new Israel. But
the fullness of the kingdom will be revealed at the Second
Coming of Christ, the *Parousia*. This is what Jesus was
teaching the disciples prior to his Ascension, as we saw in the
last chapter. But now let us look at the two passages
concerning Mount Zion in Isaiah, passages that look forward
to the last days.

Isaiah 2:1–5 and its counterpart in Micah 4:1–4 may well
have derived from an earlier prophetic source and they reveal
a high point in prophetic vision. If it were simply a political
vision we should say it was idealistic, with no real expectation of literal fulfilment. As such it could serve to lift people's
minds and energies, but only as an inspirational dream of a
Reformer's utopia.[9]

But this vision surpasses human potential. It speaks
of universal faith and worldwide peace, a family of nations of
which the centre is God himself, and Zion as the symbol
of spiritual unity. Not only will all people beat their swords
into ploughshares and their spears into pruning hooks, but
they shall never participate in war again. In his version of this
ancient prophecy, Micah inserts:

> they shall all sit under their own vines and under their own
>   fig trees;
> and no one shall make them afraid; for the mouth of the
>   LORD of hosts has spoken.

It is no wonder that Isaiah concludes the vision with the
words: 'O house of Jacob, come, let us walk in the light of the

LORD' (2:5), for eschatological vision certainly inspires new life in the present.

Whenever the prophets reach such heights it becomes a stirring vision of the end-time. The term 'last days' is not simply a form of words to denote the end of the exile from the earthly Jerusalem, but it anticipates the vision of the new Jerusalem to which we have already referred, and which will accompany the Second Advent of Christ:

> And I saw the holy city, the new Jerusalem, coming down out of heaven from God, prepared as a bride adorned for her husband. And I heard a loud voice from the throne, saying, 'See, the home of God is among mortals. He will dwell with them as their God; they will be his peoples, and God himself will be with them; he will wipe every tear from their eyes. Death will be no more; mourning and crying and pain will be no more, for the first things have passed away' (Revelation 21:2–4).

This is the Jerusalem from above, the mother of us all (Galatians 4:26), and St John the Divine is picking up Isaiah's promises for Mount Zion in the last days when death will be swallowed up, and God will wipe away the tears from every face (25:8). There is no doubt that such writing inspires and motivates life here and now, and is a powerful source of comfort for those suffering distress, sickness, mourning and death. But that is but a consequence of its basic thrust. The real purpose of such prophecy is to enable us to see that such a dynamic vision of universal faith and peace can only come from God. The proclamation of such a vision stimulates faith and creates anticipation for its fulfilment.

We felt the resurrection joy which Luke described when the disciples hastened back from Mount Olivet. Part of that joy was because they now believed in and had experienced the risen Saviour who would always be with them. And part was the joy that 'he's coming back again!' The Early Church anticipated this with an immediacy which was not directly fulfilled. They looked for it, if not in the next weeks, then certainly in their lifetime, although Jesus had warned them about date-fixing (Mark 13:32; Acts 1:7).

We've waited for the fulfilment of Mount Zion's prophecy for a long time! The Christians in Thessalonica were especially absorbed with Christ's return – the *Parousia*. Paul's teaching gave them solid instruction, corrected heresies and encouraged them to live in the light of Christ's appearing whether in life or death (1 Thessalonians 5:1–11). Solid faith in the *Parousia* must not lead to obsession or fanaticism, nor must the believer down tools to wait for it. The Thessalonian epistles were the earliest and by the time of the letters of Peter, some 30 years on, Christ's coming itself was being called into question: 'Where is the promise of his coming? For ever since our ancestors died, all things continue as they were from the beginning' (2 Peter 3:4). They had to be reminded of God's patient purpose, and that 'with the Lord one day is like a thousand years, and a thousand years are like one day' (3:8).

What was happening in the Early Church was that they were gaining a wider perspective, learning to live in the light of eternity and yet as if the Lord might come at any moment. Paul himself portrays the right attitude, looking for Christ's appearing in life or death:

> The time of my departure has come. I have fought the good fight, I have finished the race, I have kept the faith. From now on there is reserved for me the crown of righteousness, which the Lord, the righteous judge, will give me on that day, and not to me only but also to all who have longed for his appearing (2 Timothy 4:6–8).

The Davidic Messiah

When we turn to our second Zion passage in Isaiah 11:1–9 we find another prophetic vision which transcends anything that is possible on the political or even ecological scene on earth. It speaks of an ideal future king of the Davidic dynasty, his superlative virtues are the endowment of the Spirit of Yahweh, and the golden age which he brings with him is a return to the Paradise of Eden, and a reconciliation of humankind with nature.

It was with such idealism that expectations ran high with each Davidic king in Israel's history. But one after another died with greater or lesser disappointment. And when the last of them died in exile, the highest and noblest of these prophecies was focused upon an expected messiah.

In Isaiah's prophecy we find him named as Immanuel, 'God with us' (7:14), Wonderful Counsellor, Mighty God, Everlasting Father, Prince of Peace (9:6), the Branch from Jesse anointed with the Spirit of Yahweh (as in our present passage, 11:2f.) and the great Suffering Servant (ch. 53) in whom the Early Church saw Jesus as messiah and Saviour (Acts 8:32–35).

In the intertestamental period the longing for the Davidic messiah increased. On the one hand there was the expectation of a purely national and patriotic messiah to bring about the political overthrow of Israel's enemies through military leadership; on the other hand there was always a spiritual remnant who looked for a transcendent messiah from God, part human, part divine, who would establish the kingdom of God on earth (Luke 2:2, 36).

When Jesus tried to explain the suffering messiah to his disciples it caused them distress and confusion because they had in mind a powerful political figure, and in a Roman-occupied country, one who would engage in violent confrontation. We have already referred to the 'messianic secret' (Matthew 16:20–23). The terms 'Son of David' and 'Son of Man' are often used (Mark 10:33, 47), but Jesus did not publicly claim or use the term messiah.

Jesus' teaching to the disciples, and their bitter experience of his death followed by the joyful surprise of his resurrection and the descent of the Spirit enabled the disciples to preach Christ as messiah. The Resurrection was understood as confirming his messianic office:

> Therefore let the entire house of Israel know with certainty that God has made him both Lord and Messiah, this Jesus whom you crucified (Acts 2:36).

As Peter and the Early Church proclaimed Jesus, it became very clear that 'the Christ' sought no political kingdom or nationalist cause built on violence, but was increasingly seen and preached as universal Saviour who had died, was risen and would come again in glory. This would constitute the fulfilment of the highest vision of the prophets and the universal yearning for peace. This brings us to the last part of our second Isaiah passage, vv. 6–9.

Reconciliation with Nature

'The wolf shall live with the lamb' (11:6). 'If I was the lamb, I'd keep both my eyes open!' said a friend of mine. The first thing to say about this part of the prophecy is that it is Paradise regained, a return to Eden, a restoration of all humankind has lost in its fallenness and alienation from God. When the human race is reconciled to God in justice and peace, then the animal kingdom and the earth itself will regain their balance and harmony. We should include the completed picture of the old prophecy added in Micah 4:4, 'they shall all sit under their own vines and fig trees, and no one shall make them afraid'.

This causes us to ask what *kind* of kingdom is being envisioned. The Christians at Corinth wanted to know what *kind* of body we shall have in the resurrection kingdom (1 Corinthians 15:35), so others will want to know if the animal kingdom will be represented in that future Zion. Paul resorted to analogy to answer the Corinthian question, for how does one describe a body which is tangible yet immortal, palpable yet not confined by space, time or gravity?

It is significant that the animal kingdom is well represented in our passage as the plant kingdom is represented in the Micah addition, and by the fruit trees which border the river of life flowing from the throne of God (cf. Ezekiel 47:12; Revelation 22:1f.). And these fruits are for the healing of the nations.

We can expect that there will be angelic hierarchies of being, so why should not the humbler animal kingdom be represented as well as redeemed humankind? John Wesley has a remarkable sermon, 'Universal Restoration', in which he sets out his vision of a final restoration of all creation, including the animal and plant worlds.[10]

The imagination boggles in our present ignorance, but the pattern of Jesus in his Transfiguration and Resurrection opens up whole areas of reality that we can only guess at on this side of eternity. A perusal of Paul's words to the Corinthians may be relevant to this issue (1 Corinthians 15:35–58).

Our Isaiah passage is ecologically whole, and has a great deal to say to our contemporary world where consciences are at last stirring on moral and ethical issues to do with animal abuse and pollution.

The picture of Paradise regained links with the powerful section in Romans 8:19–25 – Wesley's sermon drew on this passage particularly. The same Holy Spirit which is poured out on the messiah in Isaiah 11:2 causes the whole of creation to groan and travail in birth-pangs in hope and longing for redemption in the Roman passage.

The experience of a return to Paradise was one which was taken up by the Desert Fathers and Mothers of the fourth to the seventh centuries in Palestine, Syria and Egypt, and is part of the spirituality of the Celtic tradition.[11] It is not simply that in the contemplative life of forgiveness and prayer, reconciliation is effected between the hermit and the beast, but that there is peaceful and joyful communion and fellowship between God's creatures. There is a multiplicity of simple but powerful stories, remarkably free of sentiment, both in the Desert and Celtic traditions.

Within my own Franciscan tradition the personal element is heightened because St Francis called creatures and things of nature by their 'brother and sister' titles.[12] The fierce and ravenous wolf of Gubbio becomes 'Brother Wolf', repenting of its ferocity and learning friendship with the Gubbio people who formerly lived in fear of the wild creature.

Marching to Zion

The old hymn is simple and inspirational:

> We're marching to Zion,
> Beautiful, beautiful Zion;
> We're marching upward to Zion,
> The beautiful city of God.

The last question in our long mountain pilgrimage is this: how do we get there? It is not enough to catch a glimpse of the spiritual Zion in ancient texts or even in personal and community experience among spiritual people – for the whole world is sick and needy.

The danger is that we could become exclusively obsessed by issues of peace and justice in activist and political concern as the Thessalonian Christians were by the theology of the Second Advent. We have to affirm both, live in the light of their implications, and steadily work for the common good, allowing the light and compassion of Christ to flow in and through us. So shall we steadily ascend Mount Zion.

This means that we acknowledge that we cannot bring in the kingdom by human effort. It is not simply that we do not have enough energy, but that we are caught up in the mess of the fallen world ourselves, and need deliverance from above. God alone can bring in the kingdom – and he will! But we should live in the light and joy of its reality, and in anticipation of its coming. And while we wait in hope, we must give ourselves to the alleviation of suffering throughout creation.

The life of true spirituality and holiness is wholly compatible with the loving service of our neighbours. In this way we shall be ready for our Lord's return, and whether this be in our lifetime or in the unforeseeable future, we shall be part of the eternal kingdom of Mount Zion. We began with the inspiration evoked by our first Zion passage, so let us conclude this chapter with the amazing vision of the greatest Old Testament prophet:

> The wolf shall live with the lamb,
> the leopard shall lie down with the kid,
> the calf and the lion and the fatling together,
> and a little child shall lead them.
> The cow and the bear shall graze,
> their young shall lie down together;
> and the lion shall eat straw like the ox.
> The nursing child shall play over the hole of the asp,
> and the weaned child shall put its hand on the
> adder's den.
> They will not hurt or destroy on all my holy mountain;
> for the earth will be full of the knowledge of the LORD
> as the waters cover the sea (Isaiah 11:6–9).

Prayer

Lord God of Zion:

I pray for the peace of Jerusalem and for the salvation of your ancient people. Grant to me such a vision of your kingdom that I may be filled with joy and hope; let me not be cast down by present darkness, but filled with the light of Christ. In that spirit may I anticipate his coming in glory, and work meanwhile for his will to be done on earth.

*

Action

Inform your mind by reading about some of the issues mentioned in this chapter.

Give your prayer and energies to some agency or movement which works for the alleviation of human or animal suffering, and makes our world more like God's kingdom of peace.

Open your heart to Jewish friends and visit a synagogue with a sense of reverence. Make a place for Jerusalem in your regular prayers, that the division and conflicts of that city may ultimately be caught up in the prophetic vision of Zion.

Epilogue

The Climb Ahead

We're All in It Together

In 1990, after many years of parish, university and Franciscan ministry, I responded to the call of God to climb my own particular mountain, which was the exploration of the hermit life. It began with three years living alone in a caravan in a field enclosure in the grounds of Tymawr Convent, some miles from Monmouth. In 1993 I returned to Glasshampton to continue the exploration, and now live in a hut enclosure below the monastery and vegetable garden, facing fields and woodlands.

The life has its own particular joys and sorrows, with precious fellowship in the context of solitude. Occasionally there is something approaching ecstasy mingled with experiences of cosmic darkness and vulnerability – but most of the time it is the tough discipline of training, and the pleasing freedom of faithfulness to God.

Some of my more charismatic friends (and community) wondered how my fervent and enthusiastic temperament would fare in such solitude, but I believe they now see that these years have proved that this mountain was right for me to climb!

The hermit life is rare, and although I remain stable on my patch for 50 weeks of the year, I do see a limited number of people per month, and continue the ministry of writing. I value solitude more than ever, though I am the first to confess that I owe a great deal to my community in enabling me to take this path, and to all those who have traversed this way before me. I am not alone, for I build on their teaching and experiences, and am increasingly aware of the communion of saints and angels who pray for me.

For me, this life is not the end of my life of witness and ministry, but the beginning of a new pilgrimage of prayer and love. And although solitude is the greater part of it, I am not alone. Not only am I surrounded by the prayers and influence of others on earth and in heaven, but I am making this journey for others, and for a world which is filled with loneliness, suffering and wickedness. It is a world of joy and glory too, and that is why I share my journey with others. The early Alpine climbing rope had a thread of red or scarlet running its length. This speaks to me of the redeeming love of Christ, and it is the rope by which I climb, and which I hold out to others on the perilous and joyous slopes of our journey. We are all in it together, and although the shape of our mountain may vary, the same path of love and prayer leads to the summit, which is participation in the love of God.

The Climb Ahead

Most of us have rejoiced in the verdant lower pastures of the mountain; some of us have been climbing for years; a few of us have experienced light and darkness on the steeper slopes and fancied that we have glimpsed the summit.

The last few years, for me, have made me realize how far I still am from that life in God for which I yearn. Evelyn Underhill says that we sometimes feel exhilarated because we experience something of the illuminative life and think it is almost the summit of the mountain. And there, she says, most of us come to a halt. The rest of what she says, following St John of the Cross, is the task before me and before you. I must trust that you will understand it, and resolve, by the grace of God, to accompany me on the way:

The next thing he shows us is an immense precipice; towering above us, and separating the lovely Alpine pastures of the spiritual life from the awful silence of the Godhead, the mysterious region of the everlasting snows. No one can tell the climber how to tackle the precipice. Here he must be led by the Spirit of God; and his success must depend on his self-abandonment and his courage – his willingness to risk, to trust, and to endure to the very end. Every one suffers on the precipice. Here all landmarks and all guides seem to fail, and the naked soul must cling as best it can to the naked rock of reality. This is the experience which St John calls in another place the Dark Night of the Spirit. It is a rare experience, but the only way to the real summit; the supernatural life of perfect union with the self-giving and outpouring love of God. There His reality, His honour and His glory alone remain; the very substance of the soul's perpetual joy. And that, and only that, is the mystic's goal.[1]

Notes

Introduction

1. The traditional threefold mystical path consists of (1) purgation, (2) illumination; (3) union.
2. Quoted in Peter Gillman (ed.), *Everest* (London: Little, Brown and Co., 1993), p. 19.
3. George Finch, 'The Tortures of Tantalus', in Peter Gillman, *Everest*, p. 30.
4. Quoted in Peter Gillman, *Everest*, p. 7.

Chapter 1

1. Quoted in Peter Gillman (ed.), *Everest: The Best Writing and Pictures from Seventy Years of Human Endeavour* (London: Little, Brown and Co., 1993), p. 156.
2. See Elijah's action in calling down fire from heaven, destroying groups of soldiers in 2 Kings 1:10, 12. This reference is omitted in some of the manuscripts of Luke 9:54. Note that I continue the traditional usage of the masculine personal pronoun for God, though of course God is of neither male nor female gender.
3. These quoted comments on the twentieth century are found in Eric Hobsbawm, *Age of Extremes* (London: Michael Joseph, 1995), pp. 1f., 558.
4. William Neil, *One Volume Bible Commentary* (London: Hodder & Stoughton, 1962), p. 30.
5. See 'The Historical Character of the Deluge', in S. R. Driver, *Genesis* (London: Methuen, 1904).
6. Marcus Maxwell, *New Daylight*, BRF notes for May–August 1997, p. 131.

Notes

Chapter 3

1. See Isaiah 6:1–8; Jeremiah 1:4–10; Ezekiel 2:1–3:11; Acts 9:1–9.
2. Paul Tillich, *A History of Christian Thought* (London: SCM Press, 1968), p. 1.
3. Jim Lester, quoted in Peter Gillman (ed.), *Everest* (London: Little, Brown and Co., 1993), p. 77.

Chapter 4

1. Evelyn Underhill, 'What is Mysticism', *Collected Papers* (London: Longmans, Green & Co., 1946), p. 119.
2. Robert Atwell, *Spiritual Classics from the Early Church* (London: Church House Publishing, 1995), p. 87.
3. Gregory of Nyssa, *The Life of Moses* (New York: Paulist Press, 1978), p. 95.
4. Brother Ramon SSF, *A Hidden Fire* (London: Marshall Pickering, 1985), pp. 183ff.
5. See reference in F. C. Happold, *Mysticism* (Harmondsworth: Penguin Books, 1963), pp. 51f.
6. Gregory of Nyssa, *The Life of Moses*, pp. 230f.
7. Evelyn Underhill, 'What is Mysticism', p. 119.
8. Quoted in F. C. Happold, *Mysticism*, p. 87.

Chapter 5

1. *New English Hymnal*, no. 460.
2. Frank Smythe, 'My Companion', in Peter Gillman (ed.), *Everest* (London: Little, Brown and Co., 1993), p. 46.
3. Peter Habeler, 'The Loneliest People in the World', in Gillman (ed.), *Everest*, p. 101.
4. See 'The Desert Fathers', in Brother Ramon SSF, *Deeper into God* (Basingstoke: Marshall Pickering, 1987), pp. 64ff.
5. See no. 1.

Chapter 6

1. 'A Partner in Myself', from Peter Gillman (ed.), *Everest* (London: Little, Brown and Co., 1993), p. 117.
2. Thomas Merton, *Faith and Violence* (Indiana: University of Notre Dame Press, 1968), p. 219.

Chapter 7

1. Collect for the Transfiguration, *The Alternative Service Book* (Oxford: OUP, 1980).
2. It may have been a spur of Mount Hermon, but the earliest and Eastern traditions affirm Tabor.
3. See A. J. Appasamy, *Sundar Singh: A Biography* (London: Macmillan, 1958).
4. See Brother Ramon SSF, *Jacopone* (London: HarperCollins, 1990), pp. 213f.
5. Collect for the Transfiguration, *The Book of Common Prayer* of the American Episcopal Church.
6. Information from The Christian Meditation Centre, 29 Campden Hill, London W8 7DX.

Chapter 8

1. James Montgomery, *English Hymnal*, no. 100.
2. Tom Holzel and Audrey Salkeld, *The Mystery of Mallory and Irvine* (London: Jonathan Cape, 1986), p. 297.
3. J. A. Studdert Kennedy, *The Unutterable Beauty* (London: Hodder & Stoughton, 1927), p. 117.
4. Elizabeth Clephane, *English Hymnal*, no. 567.
5. Ernst Renan.
6. *Fioretti*, Consideration 3.
7. Bonaventure, *Major Life of St Francis*, XIII, 3.

Chapter 9

1. It is remarkable that the first Christian martyr, Stephen, enlightened by the Holy Spirit 'gazed into heaven and saw the

glory of God and Jesus standing at the right hand of God' (Acts 7:55).

2. J. M. Neale, 'Christ is gone up', *English Hymnal*, no. 166.
3. J. Luke, 'I think when I read that sweet story of old', *English Hymnal*, no. 595.

Chapter 10

1. See Raymond E. Brown, *An Introduction to the New Testament* (New York: Doubleday, 1997), pp. 129, 153, 156. For New Testament usage of the term 'Messiah', see 'Christ', in Alan Richardson (ed.), *A Theological Wordbook of the Bible* (London: SCM Press, 1950), pp. 44–46.
2. Matthew 5–7.
3. The primary 'Suffering Servant' song in Isaiah 52:13–53:12.
4. Cf. Acts 2:14–41; 8:26–40.
5. See the exposition of John 4:1–41 in Raymond E. Brown, *The Gospel According to John* (London: Geoffrey Chapman, 1966), pp. 166–181.
6. *Hymns of Faith*, no. 57.
7. Kenneth Cragg, *Palestine, The Prize and the Price of Zion* (London: Cassell, 1997). David Goldberg, *To the Promised Land* (Harmondsworth: Penguin Books, 1996).
8. Personal letter from Roger Hooker.
9. This is how George Adams Smith understands it in his commentary on Isaiah – as part of a threefold pattern in chs. 2–4: (1) the idealist; (2) the realist; (3) the prophet.
10. 'John Wesley on Universal Restoration', quoted in Alister McGrath, *The Christian Theology Reader* (Oxford: Basil Blackwell, 1995), pp. 363f.
11. See Helen Waddell, *Beasts and Saints* (London: Darton, Longman & Todd, rev. edn, 1995).
12. See 'Ecology and Reconciliation', in Brother Ramon SSF, *Franciscan Spirituality* (London: SPCK, 1994), pp. 126ff.
13. Especially in Buddhist–Christian dialogue. See Thich Nhat Hanh, *Living Buddha, Living Christ* (London: Rider, 1995); The Dalai Lama, *The Good Heart* (London: Rider, 1996); Robert Aitkin and David Steindl-Rast, *The Ground We Share* (London: Shambala, 1996).

14. Quoted in Brother Ramon SSF, *Franciscan Spirituality*, pp. 131f.
15. See Sean McDonagh, *To Care for the Earth* (London: Geoffrey Chapman, 1986), pp. 8of.
16. Bede Griffiths, *A New Vision of Reality* (London: Harper-Collins, 1989), especially Ch. 4, 'The Christian Vision of a New Creation', pp. 78ff.

Epilogue

1. Evelyn Underhill, 'What is Mysticism?', *Collected Papers* (London: Longmans, Green and Co., 1946), pp. 119f.